THE
9-TO-5
ESCAPE
ARTIST

A Startup Guide for Aspiring Lifestyle Entrepreneurs and Digital Nomads

Christy Hovey

Published by Tree City Media, Boise, Idaho, United States
Cover design by Derek Murphy, CreativIndie
Author photo by Sherry Briscoe, Sherry Ann Elizabeth Photography
Copyediting by Elizabeth Day, Blue Root Editing
Formatting by Tara Mayberry, TeaBerry Creative

ISBN: 978-1-941022-06-1

For more information, visit: The9to5Escape.com

Tree City Media

For my husband, Rob.
Thank you for always saying,
"I believe in you."

And to my children, may you
all find reminders
of what you learned from me
within this book.

CONTENTS

PREFACE

Married at twenty-one, I began caring for my infant daughter while working from home as the sole proprietor of a discount cellular accessories company. I made a killing selling cellular equipment to state and local government entities by purchasing products in bulk wholesale from China. Once Amazon and eBay became popular, I closed the business.

My next project was launching a successful lawn and tree care company with my (then) husband (now ex-husband). It imploded five years later when he and our secretary left at the same time and never came back. (You can fill in the blank here. And no, they were not kidnapped and held for ransom.) After that, I acquired a real estate license and an insurance license. I receive passive income from insurance policies I've sold, and I make money buying and selling real estate.

I taught myself how to build websites and learned the ins and outs of the top social media platforms. I began speaking at local events, with great responses. I then took what I knew on the road, teaching entrepreneurship, marketing, and productivity classes for any organization that would have me.

I now own a social media marketing and ghostwriting business, and in 2014 I was recognized (along with other top performers) with a Businesswomen of the Year Award from my state's preeminent business journal. I coach business owners on how to strategically work smarter, not harder, using the concepts outlined in this book.

Over the past few years, I've been speaking at conferences on the topic of how to properly use social media for marketing, and I've landed some nice contracts from businesses and a few famous people. With constant requests from my sphere and my community, I've written what I know about entrepreneurship in the form of this book. I take deep satisfaction from seeing others become successful and turning a life of mediocrity into one that's well balanced and structured around the principle that time is the most valuable commodity.

Many mainstream workers dream about the corner office—only to find that the end result is a greater time commitment to the job, loss of self, and strained or broken relationships. What's the point of having a great view if you're miserable on the inside and have nothing to show for it except an extra digit at the end of your bank statement balance? Wouldn't a better game plan be mapping out a way to make the income necessary to live your best life and to do it in a way that you design, implemented on your own terms?

I have a gorgeous home office, painted in cool gray and dotted with framed pictures of powerful women. My favorite books line my bookshelves from the bottom of the floor to the top of my fourteen-foot ceiling. From my wide bay window, I can see a stately ornamental pear tree deeply rooted in my front yard, its snow-white petals infusing my office with the smell of spring.

I watch my children swinging outside on our white vinyl porch swing, laughing and soaking in the beauty of the season. My parents bought a house two streets away from me, and sometimes from my office window I catch a glimpse of my mom riding her bicycle, waving to me as she flies by. I'm working when and how I want to and wouldn't have it any other way. I'll never give up this view for one in a high-rise building, alienated from my family and the things that give me the most joy.

I'm a lifestyle entrepreneur. I've designed my work life around my family life, and it's exactly how I want it to be. I'm going to give you all the necessary information so that you, too, can create your ideal work life.

INTRODUCTION

At the end of our lives, we're not likely to reflect on years past and say, "I wish I'd worked more." In fact, the message from people with the wisdom of many years consistently suggests the opposite: regrets show up in the form of not having taken the time to enjoy life more—where they were at, the people they were with, the riches they already had. We all have the same amount of time every day; it's the one thing that equalizes all of us. What we do with that time is up to us.

While starting a new business requires a large investment of time, you end up with more time to do the things you want to do in the long run, and you have complete control over how you spend your time each day.

In the beginning, you're going to have to do a lot of things at the same time. There's a natural order to setting up your business properly, but you're going to be the king or queen of multitasking and task delegation. As such, I've put information in logical order but not necessarily in chronological order.

I've noticed that in the literary and business-book world there are many titles about how to think like an entrepreneur, how to have an entrepreneurial persona, and how to leverage your time and income, but there aren't a lot of books about how to actually start and run a successful business. Within this book, I've outlined how to launch a business. You'll find detailed explanations as to the how and why you should do the things I'm telling you to do. You don't have to follow it to the letter to ensure success; in fact, please don't. Be pliable and open to customizing this information as it fits you and your goals. My intent with this book is to give you the confidence you need to take action—one of the most important aspects of starting a business.

We live in an amazing time. We have access to unlimited information and all the materials we need to start and run a business. The problem is that sometimes there's so much information coming at us that it's hard to discern what information is helpful and correct and what information is totally bogus. Planning your business correctly and then running it in a way that's effective is integral to your success. As a serial entrepreneur, I have outlined the steps that you'll need to take in order to organize your business for maximum profitability, and I'll coach you with tips and tricks that I've learned along the way that have helped me in my entrepreneurial journey. It is of the utmost importance to equally balance your work life and your home life, and I will help you overcome that challenge.

In the beginning of the book, I share with you how to set things up. It's not as exciting as what comes later, but you'll save tons of trips to the pharmacy for anti-anxiety refills. Without a firm foundation, most buildings fall. Same goes for business ventures. Suck it up and clog through it, and you'll thank me later.

In the middle of the book, I show you how to position yourself or

Entrepreneurial lifestyle design means following rules and breaking a few.

your business in a place of market dominance, how to solidify your spot with kick-ass marketing strategies, and how to build a lifestyle that's designed with the end goal in mind. I also give you tools and resources to stay on top of everything without running yourself ragged. You'll be able to manage your work life so well that you won't be tempted to bail out of this entrepreneurial thing and end up working for someone else. (Heaven forbid! If you end up doing that, then I've done the opposite of what I set out to do, and I give you permission to set this book on fire.)

Near the end of the book, I give you strategies to stay on top of your game. Entrepreneurial lifestyle design means following rules and breaking a few. There are some commonalities in thinking that will help you in the long run, and I'm going to share with you how other people have successfully designed their lives. Reading about ordinary people who are living a life by design can be very encouraging when you start to self-doubt and think you have to be born in the Hamptons to be successful.

Ultimately, I hope the information presented here inspires you to live an abundant life. And that doesn't necessarily mean hoarding piles of money. Entrepreneurial lifestyle design means you're living your best life while making money in a way that doesn't steal your precious time away from the things that matter the most. I want to help you enjoy your life, your hobbies, and your relationships. My intention is for you to feel so confident in your entrepreneurial systems and so rooted in the idea of creating your work to revolve around your life that you never go back to working an eight-hour shift for someone else. Since you don't want someone else dictating the highest and best use of your eight hours every day, let's get to it.

Chapter One

WHAT IS A 9-TO-5 ESCAPE ARTIST?

The 9-to-5 escape artist understands that money can be made at any time and from anywhere. We've realized that our day-to-day lives don't have to be lived the way most people say they should be; rather, the possibilities are endless. As such, 9-to-5 escape artists tend to take calculated risks to create the life they want to live versus waiting for a lifestyle that will probably never materialize.

At its core, being a 9-to-5 escape artist means we don't rely on anyone else to provide us an income. We take 100 percent responsibility for the condition of our finances (because we know we can't rely on a job for permanence). Many escape artists integrate travel into their work design, some adopting a nomadic lifestyle or a hybrid style of bouncing from home base to a remote location for weeks or months at a time. Some have families who have integrated into this design, exploring and roaming in RVs across the country or becoming international travelers, learning about the world in a hands-on way.

As I'm doing my best to describe what a 9-to-5 escape artist is, I'm away from my home base and marinating in warm Las Vegas,

Nevada. None of my businesses are suffering for it. All four of my children are here with me, happier than they were a few days ago when we left fifty-degree weather for eighty-eight-degree weather. The college student and the sixteen-year-old have their laptops so they can stay on top of their assignments; the two toddlers have their water wings in order to stay afloat in one of the four pools at our resort.

We have a time-share and are allotted a few weeks every year at hundreds of five-star resorts. If there's availability at any of the resorts two weeks before you want to go, you simply pay a very small fee and can get a huge two-bedroom suite with a full kitchen. Few people are in the position to utilize this great perk because they aren't 9-to-5 escape artists. Spring break is in a few weeks, but we don't have to go on vacation at the same time as the rest of the country. We are living life on purpose; this is intentional lifestyle design.

Most people I've talked to here at the resort are either 9-to-5 escape artists who do this regularly or those using their once-a-year, one-week vacation allotment from their 9-to-5 jobs. If someone (an employer) has put limits on your time, it doesn't have to be that way. The Internet has leveled the playing field. Now everyone has access to free and unlimited information. No longer can anyone say they can't learn a new skill. With all of the how-to and For Dummies® books, anyone can become or create anything they want to. If you earnestly desire to become a 9-to-5 escape artist and you're willing to do what it takes to ensure a successful outcome, then do it. It's not as hard as you might think.

Common characteristics of 9-to-5 escape artists:

- » Can overcome obstacles
- » Confident (or can fake it until they make it)
- » Creative
- » Determined
- » Not risk-adverse
- » Opportunists
- » Pliable
- » Push through fear
- » Visionaries
- » Willing to fall flat on their face
- » Willing to work harder than most in the beginning

Chapter Two

THE FACTS

So you've decided you want to be a 9-to-5 escape artist, or at least you're giving the idea some serious thought. I congratulate you! Becoming a small business owner or solo entrepreneur is one of the most rewarding career choices and life changes you can make.

It's a hugely significant step because sometimes our contentment with where we are in life can become our containment. Our limited thinking makes us live in a state of small expectations. We say to ourselves that there's nothing wrong with going to a mediocre job, working all day for someone else, coming home tired and having a glass of wine or two, and going to bed just to start it all over again. Most people settle for mediocrity because they don't know any different. But in the back of your head or in your subconscious, you think there could be something better out there. You just don't know how to attain it, or you don't even know what "it" is yet.

You're going to discover what it is. It's waking up every morning and realizing that the only barriers you have are the ones you've set. You're meant for something bigger, better, and greater than where you are at right now. Don't cast your dreams aside as silly or unrealistic. And don't let others put their limits on your unlimited potential. Instead, empower yourself. Let's get started on that process by getting educated about some basic facts.

First, let's look at some facts about the opening and closing of small businesses. According to the Small Business Administration, about 10 to 12 percent of firms with employees open each year, and the same amount close each year.[1] Businesses without employees open and close three times as much, but only because it's easier to start and stop a business that doesn't have employees. Half of all businesses last five years or more, and one-third last ten years or more. You should loosely know what's going on with startups and our economy so you can know what to plan for. Without basic knowledge, it's a lot harder to ensure a successful outcome.

Another important statistic to consider is that a couple marrying for the first time today has a lifetime divorce risk of 40 percent. It's important to become educated and have a plan and a backup plan when it comes to lifestyle design. I can count myself in the divorce statistics. I started a small home-based cellular accessories business when I was raising my two children and was a stay-at-home-working mom. In addition, I ran my (then) husband's lawn and tree care company and got my real estate license while I tried to homeschool the kids. The lawn care business was hard to manage with my spouse, and there wasn't a good home-life balance, so I stopped homeschooling the kids and put them in school. Then my husband and I divorced. He got the business, and I got the kids. I was infinitely happy things turned out that way; I obviously got the better deal.

---

1   Source: https://www.sba.gov/sites/default/files/FAQ_March_2014_0.pdf.

Suddenly I became the primary income earner, which was very scary for me. I knew the decisions that I made would affect myself and my children. I panicked. I scrambled to find a job for the "security," and I was immediately hired at an insurance company. They trained and licensed me to sell Medicare supplements, and I had a quota that I had to meet or else I'd have to come in earlier and stay later. I had no time for myself, no time for my children, I was not living to my strengths, and I missed my former 9-to-5 escape artist lifestyle.

Within months I realized I had quickly moved away from my vision for myself and what I wanted my life to look like. I moved my insurance license over to a friend's brokerage, and he allowed me the flexibility to work where and when I needed to. I was given a large office and enjoyed building a lucrative book of business. Having a child with developmental disabilities convinced me to move my office into my home. This immediately freed up my time and my mind and allowed me to continue toward my goal of living an entrepreneurial lifestyle as a 9-to-5 escape artist. Luckily, when I first began moving away from what I'd initially wanted my life to look like, I recognized it happening within a few short months, and I quickly took action to put myself back on track. Had I not, I may have settled for the way my life was taking shape, and I would have been forever stuck working for someone else.

Whether you want to be a solo entrepreneur, have a partner, or operate a small business, you're doing yourself a favor by learning about becoming a 9-to-5 escape artist and expanding on skills necessary to run a business. It's inherently satisfying to build something from the ground up, rivaling the pride you feel after successfully launching your child into the real world. Both endeavors include a lot of tears, yelling, and a few timeouts here and there. But when you see your kid walking the graduation line, it's all worth it. And when you see something that began as an idea in the middle of the night turn into something that pays in actual dollars, building a business and successful lifestyle design is worth it.

The Benefits

I could write a whole book about the positive things that come from running your own business. The obvious ones are you can set your own hours. Your time is your own. You don't have a nasty boss jacking up your life with crazy demands on your schedule. If you want to work in your pajamas, you can. If you want to sleep until noon, you can (although I wouldn't recommend it until you have a decent income stream coming in).

No longer do you have to plan one vacation a year because you only get fourteen days out of the entire year to leave home. If you're self-employed, you can travel where and when you want to, and you can work from anywhere as long as you have access to the Internet—unless you're reading this book because you hope to become the proud owner of a retail store, which defeats the purpose of escaping the 9-5 restraints of a standard workday. I will not encourage you to open up a brick and mortar store. (E-commerce stores are highly encouraged, and I'm going to give you all the resources you'll need to get started right away.)

If you want to have lunch with your friends who are also 9-to-5 escape artists, you can. You can even write off half of the cost of the food if you talk about business (that alone should make you want to be your own boss). You can work in unconventional locations, like at the golf course or on the beach. You don't have to wait until you're sixty-five to complete your bucket list. Entrepreneurial lifestyle design means you can design your life around your work.

No longer will you have to look into your child's disappointed eyes as you explain why you missed their band concert for the third time because you had an important project at work that you had to complete. If your mother needs to be moved from her home in Washington to a nursing home close to you in Texas, you'll have the time to take care of her. Life will not pass you by because you'll design the life you want to live. Your work schedule will work around the things that are important to you, not vice versa.

You start every day knowing you won't have anyone telling you what to do, how to do it, or when and where you'll be doing it. You have complete freedom to structure your life the way you want to.

These very basic ideals are the primary motivators for becoming a 9-to-5 escape artist.

A Few Requirements

You'll have to work at this. It's important to note:

» If you're allergic to work or think you'll make a ton of money without having to do anything, you're just like my teenagers, and your cerebellum hasn't fully developed yet. Successful lifestyle entrepreneurs don't mind working because the end goal is freedom—financial freedom and the freedom to negotiate your time.

» You've probably heard a few inspirational talks in your lifetime. You might've heard you should visualize what you want and it'll eventually manifest itself. Or, you'll attract what you put out, you'll get what you give, and many other theories of prosperity and abundance. But the missing piece is the part where you actually do something. There are two steps to expanding your vision and breaking past barriers: you must kill your current thought behaviors that are holding you back, *and* you must take actions that will result in great outcomes.

» You'll have to work hard to manage your time properly so that your relationship with your significant other and/or your kids doesn't suffer.

» You'll need to be disciplined in order to be successful.

» You'll need to be okay with the possibility of losing money. The point of all of this is to make more money, but if you don't plan out your business properly, you could end up with less money than you started with. Some mistakes are more costly than others.

» You'll need to be okay with the possibility of losing a friend or two. You might lose one or two friends who will be jealous of your success or angry you're not spending time with them. That's okay though, because they probably weren't great friends anyway. (Don't worry. You're going to make a few more new and amazing friends.)

The People Around You

A friend invited me to a new women's lunch-and-learn monthly group for business owners. I'm always up for trying something new, especially when food is involved, and so I agreed to go with her. Upon entering the meeting room, the ringleader, a woman older than me, approached us. Calling herself a "business mentor," she had impeccable clothing and hair so stiff it didn't move when she leaned into me and pounced. "What do you do?" she asked while focusing intently on my face. I love when I'm asked that question because it's so open ended. Like, for real dollars? Or, do you mean what do I do after I've had a few glasses of wine? The possibilities for a response are endless!

Sometimes I just want to say something like, "I run a very lucrative underground poker ring" (not true) or, "I have skills! I can change the dirty diaper of a six-year-old while on a conference call negotiating a contract. Can you do that?" (totally true—my daughter has Autism). Wouldn't that be a fun way to get to know other people at networking meetings? Her tense body language as she anxiously waited for my response told me she probably wouldn't appreciate my humor.

So, to appease her, I named some of the great projects I had going on for real dollars and then paused. She took the opportunity to interject, "Oh, so you're a

> *Surround yourself with those who see greatness within you.*
> –EDMUND LEE

jack-of-all-trades and master of none." (Not that you didn't know this already, but some people have a way of being passive-aggressive so they'll feel superior with the objective of making you feel like crap. The end goal for them is they think they'll feel better about themselves. This helps them move forward in their mission to school you in the "right way" to do things—as if there's any one right way to do things.)

No, I didn't punch her in the face because 9-to-5 escape artists avoid going to jail at all costs. Being incarcerated impedes on the whole idea of freeing up your time to build your ideal life. I simply responded, "I suppose so, but I'd rather have multiple projects making me money than just one. It's sort of a basic math thing—which I claim mastery of."

Surprise—I didn't go back to the monthly luncheons, and neither did my friend. Although that woman who tried to eat me for lunch claimed to be a dream builder, she spoke the language of dream killers. I'm here to tell you that what she said is BS. You can be a master of a ton of things. And even if you're not, you don't have to be a master to be an amazing lifestyle entrepreneur and a

9-to-5 escape artist. You can know a little about something but just enough to do well at it—if you take the right actions.

Some of my best friends are visionaries. This is not an accident. Intentionally seek out others who share your yearning to be the change you want to see. Be bold, be brave, be a leader, and your friendships will naturally morph into relationships that are mutually progressive and encouraging toward your end goals.

My husband is my best cheerleader. I admit, if you're sleeping with someone who doesn't believe in you, it'll be slightly harder to achieve the goals you continually set for yourself. It's really important to surround yourself with people who support you 110 percent.

Sometimes I wake up my husband out of a dead sleep to share an amazing idea with him (which may or may not turn out to be so amazing when I'm lucid at 7 a.m.). His response is always the same, as if it's been written in his soul. He whispers into the night, "I believe in you." To become a successful lifestyle entrepreneur, you need to repeat these words to yourself daily. No matter what obstacle comes your way, with the right mind-set and a willingness to take action, you can overcome hurdles and thrive at the same time.

I have a word that I taped to my computer, and I look at it every day. It says Limitless. To me, that means there are no limits to what I can expect and achieve in my life. I was created to do great things, and so were you.

Julee Hunt, JuleeHunt International
9-to-5 escape artist

As a little girl, Julee always dreamed of being a CEO, making tons of money, traveling the world, and making a difference. She believed that if she worked hard, studied hard, and stayed focused, she would make her dreams come true. Julee aced her way through high school and college and landed a sweet job. She started her climb to the top where she was sure she would have the title of CEO.

Twenty-five years into her career, our country experienced a devastating disaster, 9-11. People responded in one of three ways. 1) They went into a permanent state of shock and became zombies; 2) They became angry and focused on hating those that attacked us; or 3) They spent more time with their loved ones because suddenly their priorities changed. As a result, business came to a screeching halt. Julee went from traveling weekly to traveling once every three months.

After several months of this scenario, the company she worked for had to make some tough decisions because their profits were dwindling and the bottom line was a dismal view. Julee received a call from her boss, who told Julee she had to lay off her entire North American team. Some were top performers Julee had handpicked herself. Julee sat down and sobbed.

For an entire year, she traveled at a moment's notice anywhere the company needed her. Julee could be in Seattle one day and New York City the next. During that year, her constant thought was, *Work harder, work longer hours, or you too could lose your job.* Did you hear that thought? *You too could lose your job.* To show you how thoughts become things, one year later that's exactly what happened.

By this time, Julee was burned out, her health was taking a hit, her relationships with her family were poor, and her creativity and productivity were waning. There was no "I" in her life: LFE = Life Feels Empty. Julee was devastated, bewildered, and without identity, and she knew she had to do something different. She started her eight-year journey from a state of burnout to a balanced life filled with love, joy, fun, laughter, meaning, and purpose. Today, Julee can't wait to get out of bed in the morning and live her life!

Julee had to take a long, hard look at herself, what she had become, and understand how she had created a life that did not include herself. This took some soul searching and question asking. Out of this journey came her new company, JuleeHunt International—Put the "I" Back in Your Life—From Burned-Out to Balanced. She is a speaker/author/coach helping burned-out executives create a balanced life that they absolutely love and enjoy. You can download her complementary eBook, *11 Ways to Put the "I" Back in Your Life* at: http://juleehuntinternational.com/11-ways-to-put-the-i-back-in-your-life and check out her burnout barometer tool at: burnoutbarometer.com. Her next book is scheduled for release later this year.

Chapter Three

EVERYONE NEEDS A GOAL

We act as though comfort and luxury were the chief requirements of life, when all that we need to make us really happy is something to be enthusiastic about.
—CHARLES KINGSLEY

Life is more exciting when you have something to look forward to. Even my little kids experience this in the form of them getting excited about things we're doing the next day. For instance, I might say, "Isabella, tomorrow we're going to clean the backyard, and then we can fill up the pool. Isn't that exciting?" She knows if she accomplishes the task, then there's a reward: awesome pool time.

As adults, our goals are a bit loftier but still just as important to define. Why do you do what you do? What are your primary motivators? If you don't know what they are, spend some time thinking about it.

We work in order to provide for ourselves and for our families, and we work because we want to accomplish something. We want our lives to matter, *and* we want to make enough money to live comfortably. If we can support our family, do something we love, and make a difference, all at the same time, the perfect balance has been attained.

Achieving this balance is not always easy, and when push comes to shove, providing for our basic needs may come before doing something we love or making a difference. The sobering facts speak for themselves. As of 2014, the federal government defined the poverty line as a family of four earning $23,550. About 50 million Americans are living at the poverty line, and 47 million of them are receiving food stamps. The median household income in the US in 2013 was $51,759.

Single women with children and women of color are more likely than men to be living at the poverty line. According to the National Women's Law Center, nearly six in ten poor adults are women, and nearly six in ten poor children live in families headed by women. Women working full time, year-round were paid .78 for every dollar earned by their male counterparts.[2]

Life happens. With 40 percent of marriages ending in divorce, it's important to have a contingency plan. Women are more likely than men to have a huge income drop after divorce and usually experience a decline in quality of housing after divorce.

Being underemployed makes housing defaults 5-13 percent more likely, and unemployment triples these numbers.

There is no fail-proof guarantee you'll have stable, long-term employment and financial security (unless your last name is Hilton). Job security is a fallacy. The only assurance you have is that you are in complete control of your financial and economic destiny. The Great Recession that began in 2007 is proof that the economy

---

2 Source: www.nwlc.org/our-issues/poverty-%2526-income-support/data-on-poverty-%2526-income

can quickly shift. Yet, during this time, savvy entrepreneurs forged ahead and thrived.

Successful 9-to-5 escape artists set their own path, adjust to evolving markets, and roll with the punches. Many workers are no longer content with the standard 9-5 workday. Lifestyle design has changed the way workers view how and when they want to work. Going to a job site in exchange for a paycheck is no longer as desirable as being able to integrate work around a flexible schedule.

A new work style has emerged from this generation. When surveyed, 45 percent of millennials prefer workplace flexibility over pay.[3] Thirty percent of companies have lost 15 percent or more of their millennial employees over the past year because they're seeking greater independence.

The good news is that becoming a 9-to-5 escape artist is possible for everyone. It doesn't matter where you grew up, if you're single or divorced, male or female, young or advanced in years. You can design an amazing life.

The Millennial Generation has learned to be two things during the recession: resilient and nomadic. As the job market improves, the level of confidence will improve along with it and cause many in this age group to reevaluate their current situation, possibly seeing value in seeking greener pastures.

—RICH MILGRAM, FOUNDER AND CEO OF BEYOND.COM—THE CAREER NETWORK

Keep in mind, however, that just because someone makes money doesn't mean he or she is going to have a great life. By definition, a well-balanced life means that all aspects of your life have been carefully examined and structured to meet your end goals. Not everyone's goals are the same, but if they're completely

---

3 Source: http://millennialbranding.com/2013/cost-millennial-retention-study/

self-focused, you're probably not living to your highest and best capacity. Consider designing your entrepreneurial goals around your health, relationships, and altruism. Giving to others can end up being one of the best benefits of being a successful 9-to-5 escape artist.

Time Is the Greatest Commodity

My parents volunteer in a nursing home every week. The people they visit don't talk about all of their greatest life accomplishments. They don't talk about what kind of homes they lived in or what kinds of cars they owned. They wistfully gaze at family photos scattered around the room, talking about and describing their kids and grandkids, who usually aren't there visiting them.

> *Your time is precious, so don't waste it living someone else's life.*
> —STEVE JOBS

This only solidifies in my mind that the main goal of life isn't to amass hordes of money. The better and happier course is to free up your time so you can enjoy the things that can't be bought, like relationships and living a well-balanced and fulfilling life. As you've heard a million times, we each have the same amount of time every day. Are you actively pursing a life with the belief that your life has a definitive end? We won't go too deep, but this calls for some self-examination. Where do you see yourself in five years? In ten?

Would you live your life any differently if you knew you had a very limited amount of time left on earth? Pretend you really do only have a limited time left. What would you do differently? I'm guessing a lot would change in your life, and the change would be implemented with urgency.

While on Instagram, I came across a woman who's close to me in age and is dying. I don't even know how I found her, but she's influenced my life, and she doesn't even know it. She has four kids just like I do, and she's riddled with many different forms of cancer. She has no hair, her eyes are sunken in, and her skin is sallow—yet she's beautiful to me because of what she says.

Through her posts, she's inspiring everyone because she's living while she's dying. Hugging her children and spouse gives her the utmost pleasure. Receiving a warm pair of fuzzy socks or a fragrant bottle of lotion brings her great joy. She savors every bite that goes into her mouth. Through her, we see through the facade of life. Her transparency gives us insight into what remains after separating the wheat from the chaff. What's most valuable certainly isn't our nametag that says VP of Operations or a certificate from a job for logging one million hours without an occupational injury.

Having more time with moderate income sustainability is the ultimate goal for well-balanced entrepreneurial lifestyle design. I don't have to, but if living small meant I could dictate how I spend my time and allowed me to enjoy every moment with my family and friends, I would do it. If I had to drive a crappy car and cram my family into a 1,000-square-foot house, I would do it. And actually, I have done it.

Be clear about what your goals are, especially when it comes to how you want to spend your time because there are lots of things you can't get back at the end of your life, and time is one of them. Chances are, as someone interested in being a 9-to-5 escape artist, you're committed to making your time *yours* and ensuring that it counts in ways that are meaningful to you. Let's make it happen!

Chapter Four

CHOOSING THE RIGHT BUSINESS FOR YOU

Why not keep working for someone else?

I had an acquaintance in the medical field, and during one of our conversations, she told me she was recently laid off after working for a company for eighteen months, because the doctor wasn't receiving enough income due to the Affordable Care Act. Prior to that, she had worked at her previous job for twelve months before they let her go because the doctor was retiring. And before that, she had worked for twenty-four months at another facility before they told her someone else had agreed to work for half of the wage they were paying her.

Although I don't work with her and don't know if there are secret reasons why she's always given the boot (like injecting Novocain into herself instead of the patients), I can tell you that this is not unusual in the workforce (getting laid off, not stealing Novocain). With so many people out of work and vying for the limited jobs that are available, employees have to work harder than they might have before the Great Recession. My second daughter recently landed a job at McDonald's. I was very proud of her after I researched how many people actually apply at McDonald's every month. My oldest was slightly jarred because in the previous year she'd unsuccessfully tried to get a job at McDonald's. (I must interject that I didn't have an opportunity to coach the oldest one properly on how to get a job right when you apply because she jumped the gun and did what everyone else does and applied online.)

Many employees also have to work for less pay than what they think they should be getting because someone else is ready and willing to work for a lower pay rather than be unemployed. With all of the new legislation affecting small businesses, many employers can no longer afford to pay for health care or offer benefits to their employees. In order to stay on top of a positive profit margin, many businesses are forced to bypass paying benefits by giving employees fewer than thirty hours of work every week.

All of these factors make it hard to support yourself and your family. It's no wonder that so many Americans must utilize government programs and subsidies just to get by. Although the root of this problem is far bigger than we need to spend time analyzing here, it's important to note that there is no guarantee that you will have your job next week—even if you are educated and gainfully employed. The incentives for becoming your own employer and boss just keep adding up.

Becoming a 9-to-5 escape artist is not going to be easy, and you'll have to spend lots of time working your business—but only in the beginning. If you set things up correctly, your hard work upfront will allow you freedom of time and the flexibility to live the lifestyle you've envisioned for yourself. If you follow the steps I've outlined here and you are determined not to give up, you'll emerge on the other side a proud and successful business owner (whatever that looks like to you). Success to me is freedom and time to choose whatever I want to do with my day. Success to you might be a monthly dollar amount. Success is in the eye of the beholder, not what society tells you success is.

Personalize Your Choices

The answer to what kind of business you should choose needs to be personalized to your individual dreams and goals. Some people will tell you to do what you love. Others will tell you to do what pays out at the highest possible rate with the least amount of effort. My suggestion falls somewhere in the middle. Obviously, you don't want to pursue a business doing something that you already know is not appealing to you and you'll hate. That'll make it a little hard to get out of bed in the morning and cause burnout very quickly. Alternatively, you don't want to pursue something where you'll have to invest exorbitant amounts of time or money and the return is minimal (but remember, you'll have to invest a lot of time in the beginning of your startup).

If you're selling a product, make sure you are able to make at least 50 percent of the markup if you must purchase inventory. If you don't have to store and purchase inventory and you are using a direct-ship model, the percentage can be much lower because you aren't storing lots of product in your garage.

The service and consulting industry can be very lucrative, but you must keep in mind that there is only one of you, and you'll have to duplicate yourself in the form of employees to grow your business. If this is not something you want to integrate into your business model, you'll have to keep in mind that your income will be limited to how many hours you can bill in a day.

I've done both models and have found value in both. In the mid-1990s when I was twenty-one, I started my first business. This was before the explosion of the Internet and online purchasing, so I had an advantage at the time. I purchased cellular cases, batteries, and other cellular accessories from China at ridiculously low prices. I then sold these accessories in bulk at a 500 percent markup to my local state and federal government entities. I did well for many years, until the wholesalers realized that they could sell directly to the consumer over the Internet.

My (ex) husband lost his job around that time, so I focused on our lawn care company. This was also quite lucrative after we discovered that we could bill $50 to spray chemicals that cost us $2 on customers' lawns. We also had a mowing division, but after much blood and tears, we realized that paying employees, paying dumping fees, and maintaining a $20,000 piece of equipment was causing us to go into the red.

We quickly dumped the mowing portion of the business and focused on the service side with the chemicals. It was a no-brainer. This business did very well up until we divorced. Although the business was not the direct cause of the divorce, I did learn a few things about owning a business with your spouse. I would definitely suggest that if you are moving in that direction, you think long and hard about it. I know a few couples that are long-term successful business owners, but the most successful couples I know don't work together in the same business, or if they do, they work in different divisions so as to avoid conflict and have a little bit of separation during the day.

So what do your friends say you're great at? What are you always getting complimented on? As an example, my friend Jade is always making gorgeous vintage jewelry and has an eye for vintage style. She can sew like no other and began to re-cover furniture for friends and family. She now sells her vintage jewelry on Etsy and is a consultant for realtors when they need a home staged.

She can make any chair look brand-new and is in high demand for her sewing skills.

Another friend of mine, Diane, is Laura Ingalls incarnate in a modern, enviable way. She owns an acre parcel and grows all of her own veggies for her family of six. She lives a purely organic lifestyle and began to make her own soaps and lotions in lieu of having to buy them at the store. She now sells her wares to local shops and is working toward online expansion.

Service-Based Business

This is a businesses model where you or your employees will provide a service to your customers or clients. There are so many businesses that fit into this category, including but not limited to:

- » Accounting/bookkeeping
- » Business consultant
- » Childcare provider
- » Copywriting and proofreading
- » Healthcare consultant
- » Internet research
- » Lawn care provider or spider abatement
- » Mobile marketing consultant
- » Personal shopper
- » Pet grooming
- » Pet sitting
- » Private investigator
- » Professional stager or organizer
- » Seminar promoter
- » Smartphone repair
- » Social media consultant or social ghost
- » Software trainer

- » Translator/interpreter
- » Tutor
- » Virtual assistant
- » Web designer

As companies are forced to meet the Affordable Healthcare Act's mandates, they are keeping costs down and turning to clients for niche work. There is a rapidly expanding market for freelance workers. Check out Freelancer.com for lots of ideas.

Web-Based Direct Sales

In this business model, you usually don't have to keep an inventory other than what you use to demo to potential customers. You usually have a catalog for sales, and a web presence is available for consultants. If you implement leverage by recruiting and having a downline, you can make passive income when the people you've recruited sell the product. Leverage simply means you are using other people to expand your reach or effectiveness. Corporate America uses leverage in the form of employees, with the exception that a manager does not reap the benefit of the team (the company does). 9-to-5 escape artists involved in web-based direct sales make money when anyone on their team makes money. Direct-selling companies include but aren't limited to:

- » Arbonne
- » Jamberry
- » Premier Designs
- » Scentsy
- » Tahitian Noni
- » WineShopAtHome.com (This one sounds awesome!)

This model has built-in supports, materials crafted to ensure your success, and usually doesn't require inventory sitting in your garage. Most of these companies direct-ship right to your customers and pay a commission on direct sales and also a commission from your downline sales (the people you've recruited to sell under you). You can check out more by visiting the Direct Selling Association. They have very extensive lists, and it's a great place to get information on companies you may be interested in representing (www.dsa.org).

Within this model, here are some questions to consider:
» If your product is consumable, what is the life cycle of your product?
» If it is not consumable, how will you get repeat business?
» When will customers need to purchase again? Three months? Six months?

Scentsy, the company that began in someone's garage here in my city and now boasts numerous employees and a gorgeous multi-million-dollar plaza two miles from my home, has a great business model. They make your house smell amazing with their scented wax, and they know you'll be so addicted to the praise lavished upon you by your friends and family (because your house smells so dang good) that you'll get those suckers on auto-ship every month. I may or may not be talking about myself here.

Repeat orders keep consultants happy and in business. If you find a whole bunch of repeat customers, you have a great stream of income from simply servicing those whom you already have a relationship with. Leveraging your time is the key here. Franchising costs too much to start up (look up how much a McDonald's or

Subway business costs—I think you might freak out). It could take twenty years to pay back all of the costs associated with a franchise.

I'm not even going to talk about retail sales. It's highly unlikely you'll be able to escape a retail store. It's very hands-on, and I just don't want to encourage you to consider it as an option to your end goal of being a 9-to-5 escape artist.

So, you can:

A. Disregard what I just told you and sell retail. (You'll have to keep inventory at a brick and mortar location, and I won't see you at the airport anytime soon.)
B. Direct sell. (No inventory.)
C. Sell your time. (Provide a service.)
D. Do e-commerce. (You sell a product on your website, and someone else fulfills the order and ships it for you. More on this later in this book.)

Larry Lim, Tahitian Noni® Millionaire
9-5 escape artist

Larry Lim's resume is impressive. He served in the US Army for 28 years and retired as a Lt. Colonel. He then went on to become one of the first licensed trainers for Franklin Quest (now known as the Franklin-Covey Leadership Institute) and was certified as a PDP (Professional DynaMetrics Programs) Administrator and Sylvan Learning Systems trainer. Becoming a specialist in human behaviors, learning and productivity tactics, and personality profiling helped Larry create a thriving management consulting business.

For 15 years Larry provided training and consulting in the areas of team building, conflict resolution, communication, leadership, and other related topics. He also taught marketing and entrepreneurship classes at universities in Hawaii and in Idaho. Although he experienced immense professional success, he still contemplated whether or not what he was doing on a day-to-day basis was meeting his life expectations. He says, "My main concern was not having residual income. I was only paid as long as I was working. I also had a few goals that I wanted to achieve but didn't feel I was getting any closing to accomplishing them."

His goals were:
1. To be able to support his three children throughout their college years.
2. To be able to care for his aging parents, both financially and to be able to spend lots of quality time with them.
3. To be completely debt-free.
4. To be able to retire with the same income and current lifestyle.

Then one day, someone introduced him to a multi-level marketing distribution model offered by Morinda, Inc. for Tahitian Noni Juice. Larry was skeptical of the business but enjoyed the product. One full year went by before Larry actively began working the business after attending a Noni conference. There he met regular people who had become millionaires simply by putting in the time and effort to build their businesses. Larry knew he had the skill set to do the same.

Larry scheduled his Noni business around his life, enjoying the flexibility of working when and where he wanted to.

Larry's neighbor saw the benefits of the product and the business model. This person had connections in Japan, and shared the business there. Now Larry has 30k+ distributors under him in 17 different countries, all of whom he receives residual income from. To him, the greatest benefit of being a 9-to-5 escape artist is, "Having control of my life and being able to do whatever I want to do whenever I want to do it." He's still building his business and living the life of his dreams.

You can read more about Larry Lim in the book, *Noni Millionaires* by Janice F. Ayre & Ansel E. Gough.

Where will you work?

Where do you want to work, and in what location will you be the most productive? It sounds like a simple question, but the answer will define your future productivity and work capacity. I love working in my home office, but I also love working remotely. Both have their advantages and disadvantages, with working away from home in remote and exotic locations being a huge draw for me.

A characteristic that 9-to-5 escapes artists share is the ability to work nomadically. Self-proclaimed digital nomads sustain their lifestyles by staying connected to a somewhat stable infrastructure, so a stable Internet connection is required. Travel is easy for a digital nomad because there's no requirement to stay in one location, although most choose larger cities over more remote ones solely for optimal access to the web.

Although you may be a traveler, it's still necessary to conduct a predictable routine. Strong and stable work habits are of primary concern and of the utmost importance when staying on top of and overseeing your business.

Digital nomads and 9-to-5 escape artists have forced self-paced productivity to the top of the conversation list. In order to meet the growing demand for community digital workspaces, progression toward the creation of co-working and office-sharing space has exploded. Freelancers still want human interaction and a place to boost creativity and productivity. Commercial developers are listening to the new market, and a new workspace is morphing to keep up with us.

Sometimes, home life and work life are too closely connected. Especially when you're an expat and traveling. If you add kids into the mix, it's even harder to accomplish the tasks that are sometimes necessary to keep your business flowing smoothly. A dedicated workspace usually helps create the distinction between work time and play time, but what if your surroundings don't allow for it? Co-working spaces are the answer.

Across the US and even in not so well-known places, office-sharing facilities are cropping up at an exceptionally fast pace. In these locations, accessibility to phone and fax booths, printers, scanners, and conference rooms are now expected amenities. Many offer daily rates, and if you're planning on being at one location for a while, monthly memberships may be available. Collective office space usually brings down the overall price of a building, as usability per square foot is higher, with the cost savings trickling down to users.

Even if you have your own dedicated office space, you might want to consider office sharing and co-working. Batching your tasks and optimizing your time becomes top priority when you're renting space by the hour. Distractions are controlled, and sometimes surrounding yourself with likeminded people can lead to higher productivity and possibly new business ideas due to brainstorming with those who share your 9-to-5 escape artist lifestyle vision.

If you're working remotely, you might want to consider loading a few apps on your smartphone.

Helpful apps when working remotely:

» **SpeedSmart** app checks your Internet speed. Digital nomads are usually dependent on a good Internet connection, and this app will prevent lots of frustration.

» **RingCentral** is a cloud-based phone and fax system for businesses, which also has an app available. (I'll be talking bout RingCentral in detail later.)

» **Every Time Zone** is a world clock app that will help you make sure you're on top of the correct times across the world.

» **XE Currency** will help you stay on top of currency rates and conversion. It will work offline, and it's especially useful when traveling through a location with sketchy Internet.

» **Trail Wallet** helps you organize spending by country, and you can set daily budgets to prevent overspending. It also estimates cost of living (and working) in different locations.

» While in a foreign country, communication and language barriers can sometimes be an issue. Try **Google Translate**. Also, **iTranslate Voice** allows travelers to say a phrase into the app and have the translation spoken back. The app's AirTranslate feature connects two users wirelessly so they can communicate in their native languages and conduct a real-time translated conversation. (For situations in which you're trying to communicate with someone who does not have the iTranslate Voice app installed, **iVoice Translator Pro** acts as a double-sided translation service, allowing the other person to speak back to the app. Other apps share this capability, but iVoice has a more user-friendly interface for displaying these translated conversations.)

» **Word Lens** can snap a photo of written text, menus, and street signs in a foreign country and translate them into the user's native language. **Word Lens** was recently acquired by Google for a planned integration into the **Google Translate** service. The app supports translations in English, Russian, Spanish, French, Italian, German, and Portuguese.

» For business travelers who venture into Asia frequently, **Waygo** picks up where **Word Lens** leaves off. Waygo is the only app that offers instant visual translation of Chinese and Japanese characters, two increasingly important languages in global business today. The app will be offering Korean translation support soon.

» For times when it's more effective to use local colloquialisms rather than a direct translation, the **iStone Travel Translation** app includes a database of more than 300 daily phrases in a wide variety of languages.

» With **PrivateInternetAccess.com**, you can ensure when you make online purchases your payment information will be safe. This app uses an encrypted VPN and a private IP address.

» When you're away from home, **EarthClassMail.com** will scan your mail and forward it to the email address of your choice. They also offer package-signing services and can deposit checks for you.

Can't find an office-sharing location? Try visiting **Workfrom.co** to discover the best coffee shops, bars, and cafes for co-working in select major cities. Just type in the city in the search bar. Users rate each location and report whether or not the WiFi is reliable.

Within a half mile of my home base sits a new facility that caters to small business owners and digital nomads. The building boasts a co-working office, a coffee, wine, and beer bar, free WiFi, and conference rooms. I love going there to work because I'm around people with the same vision and get to work in a fun and trendy environment. Do I get a lot done? It depends. It mostly serves as a way to shake me out of my normal routine and do something different and connect with likeminded people.

Aside: If You're Set on Opening a Retail Store or Restaurant

If you have your heart set on opening a retail store or restaurant, you should visit your local planning and zoning department to see what is happening in the next year in your desired location. I highly advise against opening any brick and mortar store. It's an all-encompassing venture and truly doesn't allow for a quick escape or a nomadic lifestyle.

If you feel a brick and mortar storefront is absolutely necessary, you can subscribe to your local Business Review newspaper to stay on top of what's going on in the retail and business sector within your community. In my state, the go-to business paper is the *Idaho Business Review.* I receive an edition every Friday with articles about what's trending in our state for businesses, new business filings, and other pertinent information related to business in my home state.

Remember that you'll probably have to plant yourself at the location for a while. There's nothing wrong with this business model if you are passionate about your business idea, but you won't have as much flexibility to work remotely or go on vacation for the first year. Most of these businesses require the owner(s) to have hands-on experience within the company and work in the trenches to determine what's working and not working. Many business owners also need to observe daily interaction between employees and customers to ensure the employees are representing the brand, since the employees are just as important as the product in a retail or restaurant environment.

Have you had a bad experience with a non-chain restaurant? I certainly have. New restaurants are notorious for slow food preparation, inexperienced and flustered employees, and constant menu variations. It's really hard to stay in business unless all of these key elements are properly implemented. Not to mention getting new people in the door is beyond difficult when we are all creatures of habit and tend to visit restaurants with proven track records. With that said, it *can* be done. Many culinary entrepreneurs are successfully opening up restaurants every day.

Brick and mortar stores are a hard deal. With so many big-box retailers and chain restaurants taking over the world, it's really hard to compete against them unless you have an amazing niche.

In my city, we have quite a few microbreweries popping up (lucky us!). One of these beer innovators is Sockeye Brewery. Sockeye is taking over the nation, with their stout becoming one of their fastest-selling products, outpacing the former national best seller at an exponential rate. These guys just followed their passion of making beer, and now they're turning that passion into a product that's competing with beers that previously held market dominance. I'm not sure if they're 9-to-5 escape artists, but they make beer, so that's just as awesome.

Consider whether or not opening a retail store or restaurant fits your goal of entrepreneurial lifestyle design and your 9-to-5 avoidance objective. I'm in the camp that says run away from those notions as fast as possible. So don't say I didn't warn you.

Identify Your Personality Type and Your Strengths

One day a week, I wake up insanely early and go to my beloved writers group at 5:30 a.m. Why do I do this? Because I meet the most creative, fun, and amazing people. And I truly love getting to know different kinds of people. I know I am a people person. My stepdad was a professional personality profiler for Fortune 500 companies, and I have taken more personality tests than I can count.

The discussion of personality tests came up in my writing group because one of the writers uses personality tests to profile her fictional characters to make sure she writes with continuity (which is brilliant, by the way). A psychology major in the group just so happened to have a link to a free Meyers-Briggs personality test, so just for fun, we all spent five minutes and took it and showed each other the results. (Go to www.humanmetrics.com/cgi-win/ jtypes2.asp if you would like to take it).

In this particular test, I am an ENFJ (see one description at www.personalitypage.com/ENFJ.html —there are many out there), an extroverted intuitive thinker, which basically means that I am a people person, and I can read and respond to people really well. It also means I can see the big picture but sometimes get bored on the journey. Knowing how you tend to be is extremely helpful when you are goal setting and holding yourself accountable. But I would like to caution everyone here that just because you have been profiled or typed a certain way doesn't mean you can't change, grow, or overcome.

The beauty of life is that you can decide who and what you want to be and what you want to do with your life. Play up your strengths, work on your weaknesses, and find someone you admire to mentor you along the way. I hate the saying "find yourself" because you are constantly evolving. I like "create yourself" better. But be careful not to become too self-focused; make sure you are bringing your loved ones along with you on your journey. Your gifts are best used in the capacity to make the world around you a better place. How are you using your strengths to create an abundant life for yourself? If you don't know what they are, take some time to find out!

Another test I have taken is the Gallup strengths finder (GallupsStrenghtsCenter.com). This is an interesting personality test because it gives you a list of your top strengths. The concept behind this is that if you know your top strengths, you will play to them and not to your weaknesses.

I have a low patience level, so answering all of the questions was a little tedious. Luckily, it only takes about fifteen minutes, so I pushed through all of the questions. When you take these tests, you aren't supposed to think about your responses; you're just supposed to choose what you would normally gravitate to without too much thought.

There are two questions on a graph, and you have to choose whether you are neutral or if you lean toward one statement over the other one. Some are really hard to choose between, such as: "I hate messy people" and "I avoid dishonest people." I wanted to strongly agree with both points, but I couldn't. So I chose "I hate messy people" (sorry, it's true). These are the kinds of things it's important to realize about yourself, as they can play a significant role when setting up your work environment and work relationships. The more you know about your strengths, preferences, and personality traits, the more you'll be able to play to and build on your greatest assets.

Becoming a Digital Nomad

Digital nomad has been a trending buzzword for the past few years. In a few years, there will be a different trending word to describe what 9-to-5 escape artists have been doing for a long time. Digital nomads are people who leverage telecommunications technologies (the Internet) to work, and they generally conduct their life in a nomadic manner. Many people aspire to be digital nomads, but it requires planning, discipline, and patience to attain the lifestyle of someone who can successfully work from different locations.

There's a slight difference between digital nomads and those who claim location independence. Many digital nomads live on smaller budgets and boast very few possessions. Those who fit in this category can usually survive on less than $1000 a month and are limited to living in Southeast Asia and other low-cost destinations.

Living in these low-cost areas will give you an excellent quality of life. You'll have to make more if you're supporting a family, but you'll work less than you would have to in a western culture. Digital nomads usually build up their business and their skill set and then move into complete location independence, usually having a home base to return to.

You can either start a business from scratch or buy into a business that's already making money. Just do an online search for jobs or contact a business broker who can send you in the right direction (also see www.flippa.com, www.businessbroker.net, www.ebay.com/sch/Websites-Businesses-for-Sale-).

As an alternative to jumping right into business ownership, freelancing is a great way to get your feet wet until you get the hang of working nomadically. When you feel confident in your skill set, you can start a business and leverage your time hiring out independent contractors.

There are hundreds of jobs that might fit in the digital nomad category. Here are a few you might consider:

- » Affiliate marketer
- » App or software developer
- » Blogger
- » Content writer
- » Document translator
- » eBook formatter
- » Graphic designer
- » Insurance agent
- » JavaScript engineer
- » Photographer
- » SEO link builder
- » Social media consultant
- » Transcriptionist
- » Virtual assistant
- » Web developer

Go online, Google "digital nomad jobs," and you'll find hundreds of suggestions and ways to procure business that enables you to live a life not tied to one location. I think you'll be surprised at the unlimited opportunities available to you. All you have to do is take the plunge!

Chapter Five

YOUR BUSINESS PLAN

To change is to improve. To change often is to perfect.
—FRANK UNDERWOOD, *HOUSE OF CARDS*

A business plan is necessary if you're trying to attract investors and can be a guide for you and your employees to loosely follow so you don't get lost in the process. A business plan is based on the unknown. You can follow a standard business plan, but remember, this is your unique business, and you've never done it before. It should be pliable, changing when it needs to.

Everyone's heard that an ounce of prevention saves a pound of cure, but the smart people are the ones who actually adhere to this mantra and don't want to lose any skin. If you outline important aspects of your business, it'll save you from hours of headaches later.

Don't spend days on the business plan. Don't consult with a million people or compile sixty pages of research. Just write the plan and keep it close to you. When you think of something that might be useful to add to the business plan, do it. If you need to tweak something that isn't working, then by all means please do that too.

The document's not so important that you need to preserve the integrity of it; it's not going to end up in the national archives.

Always be on the lookout for areas in your business that aren't working. If something is broken, then naturally you fix it or stop doing it altogether. It seems easy enough in theory, but I can't tell you how many times a business owner has lamented to me about a problem that could've easily been solved by just tweaking something. Sometimes we're so stuck in our pre-determined processes that we forget that the end goal is always the result of the process.

You don't have to stick to a plan or feel obligated to it. If you use a list app, like Wunderlist, create a three-month checkup list for your business and add "review business plan" to that list. Tweak as needed. You'll probably find that you've learned quite a bit about your business in just three short months. During launch, you might even find that you're tweaking your business plan and systems every week. That's okay. Forward progress due to change is better than no progress at all.

Successful 9-to-5 escape artists understand that businesses become living entities, growing, adapting, and morphing into new beings. Just make sure you haven't created a monster. In Mary Shelley's book *Frankenstein*, Frankenstein runs away from his creation once he comes to the realization of the god-awful thing he's actually brought into existence. Frankenstein spends the remainder of the book dealing with the repercussions of his creation and dies trying to get rid of it when he should have just gotten rid of the thing the moment he registered what he'd done.

Writers understand the saying, *kill your darlings*. In essence, it means never get too attached to your words that you're unable to remove them from the page. The same goes for your business ideas. You should never become so attached to an idea or system that you end up losing something more important. Like turning a profit. Like important relationships. If you do periodic checkups, you won't have anything to worry about.

Sometimes we're thrown into entrepreneurship before a business plan has been written. That's okay! Out of sheer necessity, sometimes the work comes before the plan, and you've started a business without even realizing it because you needed to eat. It's never too late to write a business plan.

Many aspiring 9-to-5 escape artists don't have a BA in Business Administration and don't have a clue how to write a plan, so don't feel bad. You can still claim BA—you're a Bad Ass for taking a risk and starting your own company.

Here are some basic questions you should be answering on paper:
» How will customers find me?
» What does the product or service I'm offering look like when it's done?
» What problem does my service or product solve for someone? Is it a real problem? And if so, how many people care about getting this problem solved?
» What tools do I need to get this done (technology, software, specialists such as a web developer or graphic artist)?
» How fast can I get my product or service out?
» Will I have partners for my product or service?
» How will I share revenue if I have partners?
» What are the things this product or service must do?
» How will I make money exactly?
» What can I do or sell concurrently or at a future date to the customers as an upsell?
» What are the expenses?
» Who will do all the work? How long will it take?

» How will I know what's working? (List exactly what this will look like.)
» What are key concerns now and down the road?
» What needs to happen sequentially to move forward?

Helpful Resources
BOOKS

» *The Secrets to Writing a Successful Business Plan: A Pro Shares a Step-By-Step Guide to Creating a Plan That Gets Results* by Hal Shelton
» *The Complete Book of Business Plans* by Joseph Covello and Brian Hazelgren
» *The 7 Day Startup* by Dan Norris

PLACES YOU CAN VISIT FOR HELP WITH YOUR BUSINESS PLAN (USUALLY FOR FREE):

» SBA.gov and SBA district and branch offices

» SBDCs—your local colleges' small business development centers (search by state https://www.sba.gov/tools/local-assistance/sbdc)

» WBCs—Women's Business Centers https://www.sba.gov/tools/local-assistance/wbc

Mentors

Look for a mentor. You might find one on LinkedIn (be bold and ask!) or within one of your community's business networking events, such as the city chamber of commerce meetings. Approach successful businesspeople within your community (look at awards such as Business Women of the Year, Top 30 Under 30, 40 Under 40, Top 20 Business Executives to Work For in your city, etc.).

You can also check out MicroMentor.com. This website brings aspiring entrepreneurs together with seasoned entrepreneurs. As an aspiring 9-to-5 escape artist, you can describe your business and your goals. Then mentors can browse the requests for an opportunity that lines up with their expertise. The mentors feel satisfaction for giving a new entrepreneur a leg up, and new 9-to-5 escape artists can learn from seasoned ones. It's a win-win for everyone involved.

In regard to asking someone within the community to mentor you, don't worry about what people think of you. The worst thing they can say is no. Most business owners enjoy mentoring aspiring 9-to-5 escape artists and won't mind spending time discussing strategies with you. Be courteous of their time and set appropriate boundaries. No one likes a time-sucker. And buying them coffee or lunch doesn't hurt either.

Final Thoughts

Remember: the key here is to spend adequate time writing the plan but not too much time. The biggest and most important task is to just start hustling! The most annoying thing on the planet

> *Move fast and break things. Unless you are breaking stuff, you are not moving fast enough.*
> —MARK ZUCKERBERG, CO-FOUNDER OF FACEBOOK

is listening to people *talk* about doing something. Have you ever heard someone say, "I'd thought about inventing that," or, "I had that idea first!" Cry me a river. I don't feel sorry for those people because they didn't have the balls to follow through with their dreams. Do the best you can with what you have to work with right now. Don't talk about all the ways you could potentially do it—just go write your plan and then actually do something with it.

Chapter Six

LEGAL STUFF

*I could tell you, but then I'd have to require you
to sign a nondisclosure agreement.*

While it's impossible for me to dictate what you should do legally in regard to your particular business, I have a few simple suggestions to offer.

1. Hire an attorney.

If you can't afford an attorney, then pay for a membership at **RocketLawyer.com** or use a pay-per-use legal website like **LegalZoom.com**.

At the time of this printing, yearly memberships at RocketLawyer are $39. It's worth every penny, and you'll just need to skip your coffee stop for ten days in order to afford it. Here you'll find every legal document you could possibly need and access to lawyers if you need to talk with one. Not only can you complete your business documents here, you can also get your personal affairs in order. You can set up wills, trusts, and important documents that your family members will thank you for after your funeral.

2. Get your papers in order.

WILL

None of us wants to consider our mortality, but (surprise!) death comes to us all. I know, I know. A real downer conversation to have when you're super stoked to start a business, but you must have this conversation with yourself, your partner, and your family members. Don't have a who-cares-I'll-be-dead attitude when it comes to planning. That's slightly on the selfish side. You might want to ask yourself a few questions, like:

» Who is going to get ownership of my business if I die?
» How will those rights be transferred?
» Who will get ownership of my intellectual property? (eBooks, websites, membership content and videos, etc.)

PASSWORDS

Make sure you have all of your passwords listed in your legal documents, or instructions on how to access your passwords if you use a cloud application to store your passwords. If you use an Apple product, you need to give someone your password so they can access Apple's keychain for all of your passwords. If you use an app like **Passpack** (Passpack.com), you'll need to leave the password to that or nobody will ever be able to access your accounts. That's really the point of those types of apps but not helpful if you've gone to a better place permanently.

NON-COMPETE CLAUSE

You should also ask yourself if you're going to make your employees sign non-compete clauses (NCC), an agreement under which one party agrees to not compete against another party in a similar trade or profession. A non-compete clause isn't enforceable in every state and is fairly costly to enforce in states that do support them. That's not to say you shouldn't try scaring your contractors and employees to death by making them sign one. I'm all about using scare tactics to avoid a future legal battle.

CONFIDENTIALITY AGREEMENT

Strongly consider making your contractors and employees sign a confidentiality agreement to prevent them from revealing private information about your business, sharing client information with companies similar to yours, or using your client lists and marketing strategies for their financial gain.

You might have proprietary information or works exclusive to your or your business, so it only makes sense you should restrict or prohibit people who work for you from sharing it.

CLIENT CONTRACTS

Are you going to make your clients sign contracts for payment of the work you do for them? As an example, if you're starting a service-based business like web design or consulting, you may want to consider having your clients sign a payment agreement. I've seen lots of companies get hosed after project completion because the client stated the work was not performed as negotiated. If you have a clear contract and outline exactly what you'll be doing for real dollars, it's a lot harder for someone to get out of paying you.

Think through worst-case scenarios and try to have a prevention plan. Consider paying a business attorney a small consultation fee just to make sure you've covered all of your bases. Visit your state bar association website for referrals for licensed attorneys who specialize in business and business contracts.

3. Consider getting a trademark or copyright.

If you don't want anyone stealing your hard work and then redistributing it or copying it and claiming it as their own, you'll want to consider getting a trademark or copyright.

Trademarks and copyrights protect intellectual property. A trademark protects symbols, terms, and names that identify the source of products or services. A copyright protects original creative work, such as blog content, paintings, photographs, movies, books, and songs. With a copyright, you have the right to control how your work is distributed.

TRADEMARKS

According to the US Patent and Trademark Office, a trademark is a mark, symbol, or combination of words that distinctly identifies a product or service. The McDonald's golden arches are a well-known example. When you trademark something, you obtain nationwide protection and have rights to pursue litigation in court. You can also qualify for international protection if you so desire.

You can't trademark something generic like the word apple. I suppose you could try, but why be a copycat when you can set the trend? An Apple computer is very specific though, and as we all know, it has been trademarked and is one of the most well-known objects over the world.

You'll want to ensure that nothing else is remotely similar to what you're hoping to trademark. If you'd like to register a logo, search the USPTO website to search for similar designs to make sure yours is unique. You can search the Trademark Electronic Search System (TESS) here: tess2.uspto.gov.

Once you confirm that what you're trademarking is unique, the next step is to visit the US Patent and Trademark Office to familiarize yourself with the process: www.uspto.gov/trademark. Then you'll need to create a description of what your trademark will protect. It should be roughly four sentences long and is required at the time of the application. You'll then classify your product by getting a code, which you'll use on your application. Then you'll need to create a jpeg file showing the image of your trademark. If text is involved, you'll need to create a file for that too.

When the application is complete, you'll need to pay the online fee. Once your trademark is approved, you can renew it every five years. If you keep using your trademark in business operations, you'll continue to have rights. And really, just by using it, you've established common law rights to it. But it's a good idea to trademark something if you're worried about someone else using it.

If you want to file for international protection, you'll need to file under the World Intellectual Property Organization's Madrid System: www.wipo.int/madrid/en/forms/.

A few things can't be trademarked, like the name of a city or the name of certain holidays. For instance, Disney unsuccessfully tried to trademark Dia de los Muertos (Day of the Dead) and SEAL Team 6. In 2006, Walmart tried to trademark the yellow smiley face. Can you imagine not being able to use the yellow smiley face on social media? The nerve of some people; my life would be over in the absence of being able to use the smiley face. :)

It seems celebrities have an easier time of pulling off trademarks. Paris Hilton owns "That's hot." (I'm not using it; I'm just stating a fact.) Beyoncé and Jay-Z are trying to trademark the name of their baby. Wow.

You can't trademark single book titles, but if you've written books in a series using the same title, you can. Harry Potter and the For Dummies® books are trademarked.

COPYRIGHT

Obviously, you must first have a created work before you can copyright it. Even if you've never publicly put a song or a book out into the world, if you created it, you can copyright it.

First you'll need to fill out the form online at the US Copyright Office (www.copyright.gov). Provide the details and full contact information. Your information will be used if someone wants to contact you to use your work once the copyright has been activated. Just like the trademark application, you'll need to provide a digital copy of your work and pay the filing fee. Once approved, you'll receive a copyright certificate from the copyright office.

Use this tool to search the copyright database to ensure you have a right to copyright your material: www.copyright.gov/records/.

At the time of printing of this book, this is the link to the copyright application: www.copyright.gov/forms/.

Just because information is on a public blog or website doesn't mean people can lift content off of it. You should always post a copyright notice somewhere on your site, alerting potential blog post stealers of your permissions policies. The tiny copyright symbol at the very bottom of a website isn't really all that prominent. Put a statement on the sidebar of your website or at the top under a tab. Simply let people know that your stuff can't be distributed without permission and/or attribution.

Sometimes you can use blog content if you get permission from the owner first and give appropriate attribution.

Obviously, definitions of terms and explanations of a process are hard to creatively change so the text is unique and original. I'm not talking about that sort of thing. I'm talking about copying and pasting someone else's content in large blocks. In fact, I've heard about people hacking someone's entire book and then redistributing it under a different name. That's a bunch of crap. Don't do that with this book because I copyrighted it and have an attorney I've paid a retainer fee to in real dollars. Enough said.

If you feel someone is infringing on your material or blatantly copying it, send them a DMCA takedown notice. A DMCA (Digital Millennium Copyright Act) takedown notice is a written request from a copyright holder asking someone to take down (or disable access to) unauthorized digital material. If it happens, politely send a notification via email and also certified mail so you have proof you did it. Visit WhoIs.com to identify who the owner of a website is and how to contact them.

In essence, you'll need to formally let them know you know they're stealing your stuff. If they don't comply, you can hire an attorney to get the job done for you, but that's expensive, so make sure pursuing the offense is really worth your time and money. You don't necessarily have to have your content registered at the US Copyright Office. You just need to initiate the process by including:

1. Statement to the infringer letting them know you are sending them a copyright infringement notice
2. Who you are
3. Why you are sending the notice
4. Proof of your ownership
5. Perjury statement: "I hereby confirm that the information in this DMCA notification is accurate." And: "Under Penalty of perjury, that I am the copyright owner or are authorized to act on behalf of the owner of an exclusive right that is allegedly infringed." (By the way, that text is copied because how else am I supposed to get it into this book?)
6. Your signature

People copy stuff. Don't waste your time trying to police the world. Is it really the highest and best use of your time cutting and pasting your content into plagiarism tools all day long so you can catch some tiny outfit in Taiwan who lifted a few of your blog posts? Unless it's blatantly brought to your attention—that's a different story.

One of my blogging friends had one of her blog posts copied and reposted under someone else's name on a syndicated site. She's a good writer, so I wasn't surprised the article went viral once it was shared to a big sharing site. The article got tons of hits, comments, and likes. She was sort of upset, as she should be. Simply sending the websites a DMCA eventually did the trick, but how aggravating would that be to have written a great post and to have gotten millions of readers with no credit given to you?

It's important to note there are certain materials that are considered "fair use." Obvious fair-use items would be news, research, teaching materials, etc. You also have protections under social media platforms in that current laws allow for re-sharing on social media without having to give attribution. The courts have yet to decide whether the use of someone's original material negatively affects marketing the original.

Going to court over trademark and patent disputes can cost hundreds of thousands of dollars, so consider this before you move forward with pursuing litigation.

Final Thoughts

Getting all your papers in order and attending to legal matters can be time consuming in the beginning, but it's so worth it because it'll save you time, energy, and unnecessary hassles in the long run. Just plow through, and before you know it, it'll be done, and you'll be set to go!

> $mart Tip: If you have a WordPress website, you can use this widget to prevent people from highlighting and copying your text: wordpress.org/plugins/wp-copyprotect/.

Chapter Seven

MONEY

Making money is art. And working is art.
And good business is the best art.
—ANDY WARHOL

By definition, an entrepreneur is someone who sets up a business and assumes risk by doing it. As an aspiring 9-to-5 escape artist, you need to be smart and proactive about your business to make sure your business operates smoothly and professionally. Expenses are a part of that risk. It's hard knowing what your exact expenses will be. You've probably forgotten something, and that's okay, but in order to create a lucrative business, you'll need to project your expenses against your income to ensure success. You don't want to be caught with your pants down.

Here's a basic list of likely expenses to get you started:
- » Accountant or TurboTax software
- » Accounting software (QuickBooks, for example)
- » Advertising fees
- » Business cards

» Business filing fee
» Checking account fees
» Client management software
» Cloud project management software (Basecamp, for example)
» Computer
» Digital camera (if you need to take pictures of your stuff)
» Docusign for electronic signatures
» E-commerce software or tools (if you plan on selling things online)
» Fast Internet
» Filing cabinet
» Graphic designer for a logo (or hire a college student to do it for cheaper)
» Insurance premiums
» iPad or laptop for portable working
» Lawyer or subscription to RocketLawyer.com
» Letterhead
» Licensing fees
» MailChimp account (free up to 2,000 names)
» Office software (Office 365, for example)
» Paper products (paper, mailers, envelopes, thank-you cards, manila folders)
» Payroll taxes (if you plan on having employees)
» Phone answering service (RingCentral, for example)
» Postage
» Printer/scanner and ink
» Projector for presentations
» Smartphone
» Social media posting software (Hootsuite, for example)
» Trademark fee

> » Website (an e-commerce website might crash, so you'll need a strong server)
> » Website hosting

Raising Capital

Raising capital can be a big concern for new and aspiring 9-to-5 escape artists. The old adage is true that you have to have money to make money. Not tons, but enough that you can set up your business appropriately. It's not advisable to refinance your house or sell a kidney. You have other options.

I have an acquaintance who started a business with a friend. The friend had a good heart and was anxious and eager to work in the business, but she was dead broke. When the two of them would have to pony over some cash for basic and necessary expenses, the broke girl was unable to cover her share. Driving places for the business was difficult because she didn't have enough money to pay for her own gas.

Money isn't the most important thing in life, but it's reasonably close to oxygen on the "gotta have it" scale.
—ZIG ZIGLAR

The broke girl caused a lot of stress for her business partner because she didn't fully disclose how bad her financial situation was to start with. Everything came to a head when a dispute erupted over a $20 expense that the broke girl couldn't pay. She couldn't even think of a creative way to come up with the money (plasma donation, anyone?).

In all seriousness, it's extremely difficult to begin a new venture if you're cash-strapped. Necessary and customary expenses need to be factored into the business plan with a means to pay them. You can't secure a web domain with an IOU. Take a hard look at how much cash you need and develop a plan to secure it. Can you creatively come up with some extra cash? I think you'd be surprised at how resourceful you can become if you try hard enough. And remember, there's always donating plasma.

The first place you should go looking for money is the bank where you hold your personal accounts. They want your business, and you've already proven your stability by maintaining an account there. Obtaining a business loan might be easier than you think. Smaller banks and credit unions are more apt to give chances to new business owners than larger banks are.

The banks are going to look at whether or not your business is viable and you are competent. This means good credit history and a proven ability to pay back the loan. If you don't have any assets as collateral, you're not a strong candidate for a loan, but having limited assets doesn't disqualify you as a borrower in and of itself. You can prove yourself competent by providing every document that the lending officer asks for and by being very thorough.

Customarily, in order to begin the process to obtain a business loan, you'll need the following:
   » A well-written and detailed business plan
   » Realistic cash flow projections for the year
   » Personal and business credit history for all applying parties
   » Personal and business financial statements for all applying parties (If you've owned another business in the past, the lender will ask for previous tax statements.)
   » Past personal credit and business history

How much will a bank loan you? It's really hard to say. Micro loans can start from $5,000, and the median small business loan is around $140,000.

You could borrow from family or friends, but I wouldn't advise it unless you have no alternatives. In *Hamlet*, by Shakespeare, he says, "Neither a borrower, nor lender be; For loan oft loses both itself and a friend." Taking a personal loan can cause a root of bitterness that can easily crop up if you take too long to repay the money. This is especially true if you don't pay back the money at all. That's a jerky thing to do. Don't do that.

A long time ago, a family member of mine lent another family member a large sum of money. To this day, the money has not been repaid, and both parties never speak of it. It's like we all know about the dead body that's in the basement and stinking up the house, but nobody is taking care of it. It's wrong on so many levels, yet neither party takes any action to remedy it. Benjamin Franklin once said, "Creditors have better memories than debtors."

Why is it that some borrowers conveniently seem to forget that they owe someone money? Is it because the creditor doesn't have any connections to the mafia? Isn't it interesting that in those circles there's less chance of default because the consequence is severe personal injury or loss of life? If you must borrow from someone you know, be professional about it. Draft a repayment schedule and stick to it. Give the lender interest on the amount to reward them for believing in you and your vision.

Another option is to apply for a loan from the US Small Business Administration guaranteed loan program. Go to www.sba.gov/loanprograms to learn about all of the loan programs available to you and what the requirements are for each one.

Investors

What about investors? You should find one, because great things can happen when you connect with a good one. Synergy happens when someone with capital connects with someone with a vision.

What's the difference between angel investors and venture capitalists? Both angel investors and venture capitalists that invest in private companies end up holding private equity. Angel investors sometimes have ulterior motives besides making gobs of money. Sometimes angels are retired businessmen and businesswomen who want to help others succeed. Venture capital comes from companies that use other people's money and invest it in a private company.

The biggest difference between the two is angels use their own money while venture capitalists take risks with other people's money. Angel investors don't mind investing during the very early stages of a business startup, whereas venture capitalists want to see some proof that the business is viable and expansion is plausible.

One of my favorite sites to visit is AngelList (Angel.co). This site is a mecca of angel investors (affluent individuals who provide capital for startups). You simply create a profile and then begin the process of trying to secure an investor. Make sure you've carefully outlined all of the details, as perfecting your online pitch will ultimately determine your success.

Brendan Baker is arguably an AngelList expert. Read his article on how to hustle with AngelList here: http://www.quora.com/Brendan-Baker/Posts/Startups-How-to-Hustle-with-AngelList-in-10-Steps.

Don't post your information without first learning the ropes of AngelList. You may hinder your chances of obtaining a backer if you look like an idiot. There's some serious action going on within this platform, so take it seriously. Use filters to find angels who've previously invested in companies that are similar to yours. When you contact angels, provide information to them showing your viability and your knowledge of the angel's past investments. If you can prove to them you've done your research, they're more apt to back you.

If you're trying to snag an investor, do not begin the process until you have a great website. You'd better have social media accounts under the name of the business. If you have the social proof that you're interacting with people, you'll be ahead of the curve. Investors aren't dumb. They're going to check out all of your platforms and see how you're doing in order to measure what you'll probably do in the future. Be clear about your terms. Use the following link and scroll to the bottom for a standard services financing template agreement from **Y Combinator** (use it as you see fit, the creator assumes no responsibility): www.ycombinator.com/documents.

Try to be unique. Instead of creating an immensely boring PowerPoint presentation, make a video instead. Let an interested angel know you're available to Skype or conduct a Google+ hang-out for further discussions. Do your research. Provide graphs and realistic yet optimistic expectations for growth. Ask questions and acknowledge when you don't know the answers. If you end up secur-ing an investor, I'd love to hear the backstory! Send me an email.

Your Pitch

Business coaches preach the elevator pitch. What's an elevator pitch? It's a fifteen-second line about your business you've perfected in front of a mirror. I hate elevator pitches. Nobody rides the eleva-tor anymore anyway. It's more like a running up the stairs pitch or striding along whatever you call those things in airports when you can walk really fast pitches. Most of the time they're forgettable because they're rehearsed and all about you and your business.

The traditional model says to tell someone exactly what you do in an eloquent and stand-out way. Nobody cares what you do unless you can fill a need—their need. If you offer a service or product that'll help someone do better or be better or prevent stress or whatever, then you have a memorable pitch.

If you need money from investors, you're going to need to learn how to pitch your angle. You'll need to write an executive summary explaining your business model and what makes you special. Just because you can sell ice to an Eskimo doesn't mean you'll be a great CEO. You have to have a strategy for marketing and getting your product to the consumer. You have to know who your competitors are, what your management structure will be, and how you plan to grow the company.

Savvy investors will know if you're padding your numbers, so don't do it. Give realistic but optimistic projections for growth, finances, and cash flow. Excitement and passion are great traits for 9-to-5 escape artists but not great company selling points when pitching to an investor. Let your originality and the numbers do the talking.

Sometimes you need more money to reach your business goals. Not everyone has a rich grandpa who has no qualms investing in any idea you present to him. Practice your pitch with the video feature on your smartphone. Don't have a smartphone? Stop reading this book and order one right now.

Okay. Record your pitch. Watch it. Would you buy a product or service from you? Be honest. If not, then try again. Keep tweaking your pitch until you're convinced. You never know when all of that practice in front of your iPhone video camera will pay out big time.

Crowdfunding

Crowdfunding is a new and exciting way to raise a lot of money from people you don't necessarily know. According to *Merriam-Webster,* crowdsourcing is "the practice of obtaining needed services, ideas, or content by soliciting contributions from a large group of people and especially from the online community rather than from traditional employees or suppliers." Crowdfunding builds upon the idea of crowdsourcing in that instead of gathering a whole bunch of people to share knowledge, you're asking anyone and everyone to fund your business.

When your bank account numbers don't quite align with your vision, you may want to consider using crowdfunding to raise capital. At Kickstarter.com or Rockethub.com, you can launch a successful donation campaign. You'll need to draft text explaining your product or service (your pitch). You'll need to set a goal and create a deadline for raising the funds. Platforms like Kickstarter are strictly monitored for correct representation, and you must ensure accuracy in all of your statements.

Potential donors are not investors; they are supporting you by funding your request. They are rewarded based on what you've identified as benefits to funding, but you are under no obligation to give them any ownership or right to your product or service.

The caveat is that you must reach your intended monetary goal or you don't receive any of the pledged funds. Pledges are made with a credit card or PayPal, and the card isn't charged until the project reaches its goal.

In order to reach a whole lot of people, you're going to need to employ some creative strategies to reach anyone and everyone who will listen. I strongly suggest hiring a few college students to sit on your social media sites and hammer out requests for donations day in and day out. You never know who'll see your request and become interested.

I've been involved in some really great crowdfunding endeavors, both as a campaign creator and as a donator. The most recent donation I made was to a photography artist who was trying to raise $30k for a photography book project. This guy's work was amazing; the moment I saw his photographs on social media, I was hooked. I didn't even know him. One of my contacts just reposted his request. I was happy to donate $25 in exchange for a print from his book. He reached his goal of $30k. Done and done!

Ideally, a crowdfunding campaign should target a market that would most likely be interested, but as mentioned above, don't discredit random strangers from getting excited about your campaign. Create passionate posts in advance and use a social media scheduler like Hootsuite to get your message out 24/7. Use compelling text and images. Had I not seen the photographer's work, I probably wouldn't have been very excited to donate to his campaign.

Using traditional marketing tactics like calling people and word-of-mouth advertising, combined with a compelling email marketing plan and nonstop social media blurbs, you'll more than likely easily meet your goal.

Think your numbers are too high? Think again. Some crowdfunding campaigns have hit their goals within one hour of posting a campaign.

Whether you're trying to build a prototype or fund a book project taking you around the world, you should at least consider crowdfunding. What can it hurt?

Here are a few crowdfunding sites to look into:

» GoFundMe.com
» Kickstarter.com
» IndieGoGo.com
» Social: Buzzbnk.org
» Non-profits: CauseVox.com and FirstGiving
» Mobile apps development: AppBackr

Networking

Sometimes just hanging out with the right people can help you connect with potential moneylenders. Investors hang out with other investors. If you've pitched to an investor and they've declined your offer, then politely ask them for a referral to someone who might be interested in hearing your pitch. Get on Facebook and connect with mastermind 9-to-5 escape artist entrepreneurial groups and ask for help. Read what others are saying and learning. Reach out to successful 9-to-5 escape artists within your community and ask them if they can point you in the direction of an investor willing to listen to new business pitches. You'll probably get lots of no's in this process, but all you're looking for is one yes.

Alternatively, ask an attorney if he or she has any clients who'd be willing to give you a few minutes to pitch. Accountants might also know investors or venture capitalists. You'll also want to check with your local SBA and banks to see if they offer any special financing loans, especially if you're a woman or a minority.

You could also offer trade services to potential investors. Usually they'll want to trade in stock options from your company or become vested in your business, but they might be open to trading services or products. It certainly doesn't hurt to ask. Try to think out of the box if you just can't seem to go the traditional route to secure the cash you need to start your business. This most likely won't be an issue, but you need to have a backup plan in case cash flow gets tight.

Hopefully you won't start a business that requires a huge amount of capital, and you won't get all crazy and buy a million-dollar commercial building from the get-go. If you have bipolar tendencies, make sure you first run a large investment or purchase by someone you trust. Typically, good friends won't let you do something really stupid or irrational. Frenemies might, but not those who have your best intentions at heart.

Keep Your Eyes Open

Watching your bank statements is almost as fun as watching paint dry. It's a necessary task, like taking out the garbage. View it as such, and your business won't start to get stinky.

When you're trying to hustle and create a business that results in real dollars, you have a lot of things you have to keep your eye on. It can be hard for one person to watch the finances, do the marketing, drum up cash, and answer client emails. Sometimes it's just easier to hire out tasks to people who specialize in the skill set you need and don't have time to learn.

Whether or not you hire a CPA to handle all of your accounting and financial statements, you'll still need to keep your eye on the numbers. Make sure you're getting monthly and quarterly reports or spreadsheets so you can have full access and understanding as to what your bottom line is. One document you should watch in the same manner you watch a boy who's in your family room with your daughter is your income statement (otherwise known as a profit and loss statement).

Basically, the equation is: revenue minus expenses equals net income.

Total Revenue	$200,000
Cost of Goods Sold	($40,000)
Gross Profit	$160,000
OPERATING EXPENSES	
Salaries	$10,000
Rent	$10,000
Utilities	$5,000

Depreciation	$5,000
Total Operating Expenses	($30,000)
Operating Profit	$130,000
Interest Expense	($20,000)
Earnings before tax	$110,000
Taxes	($20,000)
Net Income	$90,000
Number of Shares Outstanding	90,000

Theoretically, net income is accessible to shareholders, although more often than not, earnings are retained for future investment back into the business. Shareholders (owners of the business) usually want the company to grow versus cashing out their shares. It's important to show a healthy operating profit. This is where you'll pull from for debt repayment, so if that number is low, then bankruptcy court is in your future.

If your operating expenses skyrocket, something shady might be going on, and you need to address it right away. One of my girlfriends owns an amazing salon and spa. She has independent contractors leasing spaces, and she does very well in our area. She's an industry leader, and her place is always packed. One month she noticed her total operating expenses were up by $2,000. That might not seem like much if you're raking in the money, but when all other numbers remain the same, you should question it.

The same amount of clients had been seen as the previous month, all of the contractors were still there, and they had all paid their rent that month. There was nothing to substantiate the increase in expenses. After combing over the receipts with her accountant, my friend identified the problem. Someone was selling product and then pocketing the cash. The product was replaced, but there was a deficit when the income for the sale wasn't recorded.

Had my friend not been watching her numbers, she wouldn't have caught it for a while. She immediately installed cameras on the product and at the point of sale area. Wouldn't you know it, the next month her operating expenses normalized, and she hasn't had a problem since. Yes, installing cameras is an effective way to catch thieves, but so is watching your balance sheet.

Almost as important as the income statement is the cash flow statement and balance sheet. Ask your accountant to help you with setting these up properly, or, if you use QuickBooks, go online and find a template or a custom report to help you keep track of everything. Go to Intuit's QuickBooks website for a full list of available reports: intuit.com/accounting-reports/. If you don't have an accountant or QuickBooks, check YouTube for tutorials, using the keywords for the reports you'd like to generate.

Business Accounts

Check with all of the banks in your area to see if they offer any perks for signing up for a new business account. When I opened up my most recent banking account with a partner, the bank offered us $250 in a cash deposit if we maintained a certain balance for six months. Now that's a great deal.

> $mart tip: Check Bankrate.com to view information on the banks in your area. This is also a great place to compare mortgage and auto loans if you're in the market for a big purchase.

Chapter Eight

ECOMMERCE

*If you have the choice to have money or not
to have money, pick having money.*
—SEX AND THE CITY

Setting up and maintaining an e-commerce site and/or business is not as hard as it sounds. There are so many digital moneymaking tools at your disposal; you just need to learn how to use them.

You can use PayPal to send invoices to clients via email. Save yourself the expense of printing an invoice, paying for a stamp, and then waiting for payment. Payment is instantaneous. With PayPal there's no reason you'll have to wait forever to get paid. If you have awesome clients, they'll usually pay within a week of receiving an online invoice. You can even use PayPal's system to send a gentle reminder that you need some new shoes, so can you please pay now?

As of this printing, PayPal is free to use, but you'll have to pay 2.9 percent for every transaction under a certain dollar amount. They also offer a service called PayPal Website Payments Pro, which offers basic shopping-cart functionality and costs $30 per month plus transaction fees.

If you don't want to build a website yourself, there are many companies that specialize in e-commerce templates for websites. You can find packages that include product catalog tools, shopping-cart technology, payment, and reporting. The beauty of finding a quality turnkey e-commerce provider is you'll immediately have access to everything you'll need to start your business. Like immediately. Your only job is setting it up and then procuring the product or products you want to use it for.

EBay offers e-commerce services that are available to anyone, not just eBay sellers, called ProStores. Potential customers don't see the association between you and eBay because there's no identification to eBay. The website is accessed through a regular URL. The fee for a ProStore package starts around $7 a month, and they will charge you a small fee for every transaction you process (starting at 1.5 percent per transaction).

Yahoo has one of the largest market shares in the e-commerce merchant solutions business because of their early entry into the game. Whenever someone enters an emerging market first, they can usually ride market dominance for a while. Plans start as low as $26 but don't offer third-party integrations or support. You'll pay a monthly fee, a one-time setup fee, and a per-use transaction fee.

Volition.com is aggressively trying to lure potential merchants away from Yahoo by boasting no transaction fees, no annual contracts, and over three hundred design templates. Volition plans start at $15 a month for up to one hundred products.

An up-and-coming e-commerce player is the merchant Square (SquareUp.com). Square initially gained popularity by releasing a free portable credit card reader that easily fits into a smartphone and processes payments using an app. Square seamlessly integrates with Apple products and is now being extensively used with iPads as a point-of-sale mechanism. Square can send receipts electronically via text or fax, making the process even easier. They have some beautiful website templates and are diligently working to claim their place next to other power players in the e-commerce market.

Amazon is arguably the biggest competition to eBay. Amazon sellers receive many benefits, and Amazon promises to turn you into an e-commerce guru by they time they're done with you. According to Amazon, you'll have access to the same scalable infrastructure as Amazon.com. In all honesty, Amazon has their sights set on world domination, so it doesn't hurt to be a part of a company with lofty goals and the resources to accomplish them.

With Amazon's web store, you can use fulfillment by Amazon to ship your orders. You can also offer their Prime free two-day shipping on your website. With Amazon's payment processing services, your customers can log in and pay using their Amazon account. All of Amazon's e-commerce templates are mobile-optimized and easy to use with a drag and drop system. Visit webstore.amazon.com for more information.

As an alternative to the e-commerce platforms mentioned previously, Shopify.com caters to smaller markets. Shopify stands out against competitors because it offers unlimited bandwidth, a feature that comes in very handy. They also have an abandoned cart feature, emailing customers with a reminder that they forgot to finish their purchase. Like PayPal and Square, Shopify offers a mobile app for accepting payments and store management tools.

Other e-commerce platforms to check out include:

» BigCommerce.com
» GoEcart.com

» 1Shoppingcart.com
» ShopSite.com
» PinnacleCart.com (offers automated Intuit QuickBooks synchronization, a very useful thing to have)

Whatever system you choose, make sure it offers SSL encryption. This means your customer's personal information and credit card information will be transmitted securely over the Internet. You don't want to worry about fraud jeopardizing your reputation. You'll also need to test your site often. Make sure it can handle heavy traffic. Ask others to view your website and take suggestions seriously. Just as you'd have an editor proof your book, have someone proof your site for spelling errors, broken links, images that don't load, or pages that load too slowly.

If you want to integrate e-commerce into your Facebook page, try one of these apps:
» EasySocialShop
» Ecwid
» Shopify
» ShopTab
» Storefront Social
» Storenvy
» Volusion

Most e-commerce purchasing should take place on your website, but you don't want to miss out on any opportunities to sell on other platforms.

If you'd like to bypass storing and shipping items you'd like to sell on your website, you might want to consider using a drop shipping order fulfillment center. With this model, you simply list items offered by the drop shipper on your website, you collect the funds after your customer makes a purchase, then you place a wholesale order with the drop shipper, who then ships the item right to your customer. You keep the difference between what you paid for the product at wholesale and what you sold the product for at retail.

Using a drop shipper equals low risk for you. You won't get stuck with hundreds or thousands of products that may or may not sell. You only place an order for items when someone makes a purchase from your site. You won't be out any money for inventory nor will you have to worry about getting the product to your customer. As a 9-to-5 escape artist, you certainly don't want to spend your days bubble wrapping and shipping and tracking products. By using a fulfillment center, the only tasks you have to worry about will revolve around marketing and maintaining your business (and maybe planning your next vacation).

Check out Doba.com and ShipWire.com for your product fulfillment needs.

With a well-developed e-commerce system, you can make money twenty-four hours a day. You'll also sleep easier at night knowing you're not going to wake up to a million problems caused by web inefficiencies. Gone are the days of having to babysit the phone, taking orders. Because you've implemented a secure and professional shopping experience, you can leisurely sip a Port Royal on the crystal blue-green West Bay Beach in Roatan without worrying about your business. If you've integrated a third-party shipping source, all you have to do is watch the numbers. Can you see why 9-to-5 escape artists are such happy people?

Beth Markley
9-to-5 escape artist

When she launched her own consulting business, Beth did so because she knew she was unhappy with her work/life balance. Her job required more travel than she wanted, her kids needed more of her time, and her grandmother was moving into their basement apartment. Still, she needed and wanted to work.

A colleague had told Beth there was more work in fundraising consulting than consultants available, so Beth decided to take the leap. Business was slow at first, but with the demands of caregiving for her children and grandmother, this worked out well. As Beth's client list grew, both kids entered grade school, and her husband and mother provided support in caring for her grandmother.

For years, Beth enjoyed the flexibility of working from home. She was able to pick kids up from school and attend recitals and events and still keep her clients happy. She also appreciated the variety of projects. Over time, she decided to specialize in certain areas, concentrating her work on those tasks that gave her the most joy. She marketed her services primarily by offering her time as a speaker and trainer for fundraising and nonprofit groups, and by volunteering for boards and committees in the community, which helped her feel like she was making a difference.

Ten years later, Beth's husband, Mike, joined her. The decision was a tough one—to go from at least one stable income (plus insurance and benefits) to relying fully on the variable nature of consulting. Mike took on a lecturer position at Boise State University to help compensate, which also provided health insurance and other benefits.

While there were things to get used to, Beth and Mike love working together and having more flexibility for their two boys as they grow.

Beth maintains a blog for her consulting business at www.markley.com. She also keeps a blog of personal essays as a humorist and mom at www.manicmumbling. com.

Chapter Nine

RESEARCH

Everyone is not your customer.
—SETH GODIN

An important component of doing research before you craft a killer marketing plan for your business is identifying your typical customer. It's not realistic to think that everyone from all walks of life will want to buy your service or product. But be careful; targeting specific groups doesn't mean you should dismiss other groups that might not fit your criteria. It simply means you're going to spend the most energy, effort, and money targeting those who are *most* likely to buy from you.

It's very important to identify your target audience, but be mindful to not break your list down too much. Or, if you do, you'll need to have separate marketing plans for each niche market you've identified. If your target market is too small (under five hundred people), you've probably broken the list down too far, or you don't have a viable, sustainable business or product.

If you're at a loss as to how to start digging up information about your potential target market, begin by doing a Google search. It's a great and free place to start. See what auto-populates when you're doing a search for your service or product. Pew Research Center (PewInternet.org) offers reports on Internet use with certain demographics. Scarborough.com publishes useful data and offers some free studies. You can also visit Nielsen.com for useful information.

Obvious sources for information would be the US Census Bureau, trade associations, or paying third-party researchers to do the research for you. Don't forget about your local small business administration office and local community college. Both offer free information for business planning and development.

Want to conduct your own research? You can create surveys for free or with very little cost using survey tools such as SurveyMonkey.com or Zoomerang.com. You can dig deep and conduct interviews with potential customers for answers to how potential customers feel about your product or service. Analyze the responses and review the data as it pertains to your end goal. Use your research to make adjustments to your marketing plan. You might end up tweaking your business plan based on the feedback.

Know Your Competitors

While researching your competition, you may want to dig deep and find out whom your competitors are marketing to. Who are their customers? Is your competition overlooking a niche within the same market that you might be able to fill?

> *What people actually refer to as research nowadays is really just Googling.*
> —PETER LEWIS ALLEN

Poll people you know. Ask your friends, family, and business mentors what they think about your business concept. What gaps can they see that maybe you don't? What's the first thing that comes to mind for others when you mention your business service or product? Don't discredit any opinion but weigh it against the averages.

If you're going to do the same thing as your competitors, how can you do what they're doing in a better way? What value proposition do you offer to your potential customers, and what is your competition currently offering? Are there any gaps for you to enter the market with a bang?

If you've developed an amazing hammer and want to sell it at your own retail store, how are you going to bring customers in when most everyone is going to big-box stores like Lowes or Home Depot? Even if your hammer is state-of-the-art, how are you going to get it into the hands of your target market? If you can't answer this question, it might be better just to get your hammer into the big-box stores.

Use Google because it's a free tool that'll help you find all the information you'll need on your local and national competitors. Use targeted keywords in your search (and keep record of each search for future reference). What reviews pop up when you input the keywords in the search bar? Reading competitor reviews can give you great insight into what other companies are doing right and wrong when it comes to their clients. You'll also learn about customers' favorite products and what services they're searching for the most. Note what auto-populates in the search bar when you start typing. This tells you what Google has logged when people are searching, giving you an idea of what's most important for a potential customer.

Check out Alexa.com, a web page ranking system. You can get basic analytics for free and more advanced analytics for a fee. You'll learn where your competition ranks on the web and what kind of traffic numbers they're getting. Audience demographics are listed, including sex, education, and geographic location. It'll also tell you whether someone is browsing the site while at home, work, or school.

You can learn a lot just by looking at this basic information. When I typed in Orbitz.com, I found that they ranked 397 of all websites in the US. Females are far surpassing males as visitors to the site. Most of them have some college or no college background, yet they're browsing from a school location, so they're most likely current students. Alexa reports 26 percent of them visited Google right before hitting Orbitz, so that tells you Orbitz had a top banner ad that converted into a click. Finally, I can see websites that are related to Orbitz, such as Hotwire, Expedia, and Cheaptickets.

Wow! If I wanted to start an online travel agency, I already have some key pieces of information about my target market, honed down to their sex, where I can find them, and how they will most likely find me. I also found out who my top competitors are. Don't discredit free resources. I'm all about getting stuff for free. You don't have to pay a research analyst if you can find the information on your own.

Compete.com is another amazing resource for researching your target market and your competition. They offer comprehensive consumer behavior data for your industry. They boast that they'll tell you the "market strategies that work best in your industry, which tactics fall flat, and where to find untapped opportunities ... increasing return on your efforts." You can access these resources with their intro plan of $249. If you have the resources, you should consider this as a small and necessary investment for the future success of your business.

When you do your research, there are a few terms you'll want to be familiar with:

» **Demographics:** statistical data, including age, income, and education

- » **Psychographics:** the attitudes and tastes of a demographic group
- » **Ethnographic:** detailed understanding of a certain culture
- » **Buying habits:** how customers purchase, where they purchase, and what they purchase

Understanding Your Target Market

I suggest first creating a list of each aspect of your product or service. Beside each item you've listed, write down the benefits offered (and continue, using the snowflake method or a similar mapping method).

After finishing your benefits list, create a list of people who have a need for these benefits. Really dig deep here. If you get stuck, ask your business mentor if he or she has any more groups to add to your list. Once you have a strong list, think about defined characteristics of those you would most likely convert into a sale.

These factors should be a part of your consideration when defining your target market:

- » Age
- » Education
- » Ethnic background
- » Gender
- » Income
- » Location
- » Marital status
- » Occupation

Further considerations may be their traits and interests:

» Hobbies

» Lifestyle

» Values

Identify how your product or service will integrate into your target market's life:

» How do these people get their news?

» What benefits of your service or product are most appealing to them? When and how will they use them?

Think about your list in terms of:

» Is my target audience easy to reach?

» Can they truly afford my service or product?

» Do I really understand them?

» Have I identified enough people for me to stay in business?

Now that you have your head wrapped around who you should be intentionally focusing your marketing efforts on, you're ready to take action. Taking time to identify your target market will save you money and lots of frustration. Now, instead of plastering your city with mailers that will

> *The worst thing I can be is the same as everybody else. I hate that.*
> —ARNOLD SCHWARZENEGGER

only end up in the trash, you'll be sending mailers only to your target audience. Hopefully only a few mailers will end up in the trash (but actually studies show that paper mailers convert at a rate of 1 to 3 percent, so you may want to rethink that strategy[4]).

---

4 Source: http://dmdatabases.com/resources/interesting-articles/direct-marketing-articles/direct-mail-response-rates

Identify what makes you unique and build a platform around it. Focus your efforts on building a brand that stands apart from your competitors. You don't need to recreate the wheel; you just need to make your wheel a little different from everyone else's.

There's Enough Business to Go Around

Paige Arenof-Fenn, founder and CEO of Mavens & Moguls, says, "Attracting more customers is really about listening to their needs, not being a solution looking for a problem."

There's plenty of business for everyone. I find it laughable when someone is worried

Abundance is not something we acquire, it is something we tune in to.
—WAYNE DYER

about another person opening up a similar business to theirs. Just do an amazing job, and the business will come. There are a billion people on this planet, and I'm confident you'll be able to secure enough business to keep your family happy and fed.

Don't tell yourself there's not enough business to go around. There is; that's just a way to get out of having to work hard to find it. I grew up with the *Field of Dreams* movie. I think my family watched it a hundred times. The premise of the movie really spoke to my soul, even as a young teen, and it wasn't because I watched it over and over (well, maybe a little). **"If you build it, they will come."** Just saying it now gives me goose bumps.

If you have a killer website, create an amazing and somewhat unique platform, and work your business like a boss, they will come. Whoever *they* need to be, you will attract them. All of the big self-talk gurus have coined some law or principle around this idea. Law of Attraction, Law of Prosperity, Abundance Principle, whatever you call it, it means the same thing. If you build it, then they will come, and you will have all the business you need.

When you speak to yourself and when you speak to others, allow only words of prosperity and abundance and optimism to leave your lips. Speaking of words, I know an amazing man in my area that did a cool experiment. He filled two jars with the exact same amount of rice to water ratio. On one jar he taped text with mean and ugly words like failure, poverty, loser. On the other jar he taped words like prosperous, abundance, joy, love. Wouldn't you know it, within a few weeks the rice with the negative words had mold growing on it. The rice with the positive words taped to it looked the same as the day he started the experiment. If it works on rice, it'll probably work on you.

Wake up every morning believing you're creating abundance and joy, not just in your life but in the lives of others too. You were created for a specific time and purpose. Don't waste a moment believing you're not meant to impact your world, because according to Steve Jobs, co-founder of Apple, "The people who are crazy enough to think they can change the world are the ones who do."

Chapter Ten

MAKING IT OFFICIAL

Sole Proprietorship

If you're working by yourself or under a freelancer-type business, you're probably already doing business as a sole proprietorship and you didn't even know it. There's not much protection, and you're not incorporated. You might be comingling your profits and expenses in your personal account, but you really shouldn't.

For tax reporting purposes, it would be best if you ran your debts, losses, and liabilities through another account. Many sole proprietors choose to file a DBA (assumed name, doing business as) that's different from their own name. Then you can open a bank account under your DBA. You can use the online search tool at your state's secretary of state office to see if anyone is using the cool name you've come up with.

When you file taxes, you'll report your income with a Schedule C. Your net profit after all of your expenses transfers to your personal tax return, so make sure to keep track of everything in an easy-to-input format. There are a few apps that might be helpful for you in tracking and logging expenses on the go, including Expensify.com and OneReceipt.com (which scans Gmail for receipts).

Benefits of a sole proprietorship include simplicity, low costs, and complete control of all aspects because you don't have a partner. Downsides of a sole proprietorship include unlimited personal liability and challenges when trying to get investors because there are no stocks you can sell and banks perceive you to be less credible for repayment. In my humble opinion, you can start as a sole proprietorship if you're dead broke and want to get your hustle on. Once you've made a few hundred bucks, you should probably get an LLC done and over with.

Limited Liability Company (LLC)

An LLC is a hybrid business legal structure that offers the limited liability features of a corporation and the tax benefits and operational flexibility of a partnership. Owners of an LLC are commonly referred to as members. Depending on the state you live in, members can be one owner, two or more people, corporations, or other LLCs. You'll need to file an Articles of Organization document outlining your business name, address, and the names of the members of the LLC.

The advantages of an LLC are members are protected from personal liability for business decisions, and members' personal assets are usually exempt. That doesn't mean you can go and do something totally illegal and not get sued. It just means you have more protection than you would if you didn't create an LLC. I am always amazed when I find out someone is operating a business without formally filing the necessary paperwork with the state. It's super easy to create a company for real. Just go to RocketLawyer.com and pay the small fee to access the appropriate forms.

Partnerships

In a nutshell, a partnership is a business entity that two or more people share ownership of. The partners share in contributions that include money, property, and labor. Each partner shares in the profits and losses of the business. A partnership agreement is created by identifying how products and services are made, how profits are distributed, and how disputes are handled, among other important details. It would not be advisable to create a partnership without having a partnership agreement firmly in place. I recommend having it signed by a notary and maybe even recorded at your county recorder's office for good measure.

There are three types of partnerships:

» **General:** Profits, liability, and management duties are divided equally between partners, or you can assign different distributions as long as everyone has agreed to that.

» **Limited:** Limited liability partnerships are slightly more complex than general partnerships. They protect the partners from certain liabilities as well as limit management decisions based on each partner's investment percentages. If both parties agree, sometimes it's best if the split is 51/49 percent to ensure you don't arrive at an impasses. You might have to flip a coin for that one.

» **Joint Ventures:** These mimic general partnerships with the exception that they are usually for a limited time or for a specific project.

There are definite advantages to having a partnership. They're easy and inexpensive, and it's nice to have multiple individuals sharing in the success of the business. You can pool resources both in capital and in brains. Having more than one person working on the business helps with efficacy, and it means the stress is distributed evenly. You both might get ulcers, but at least you'll be able to talk about it with each other.

I find it helpful to have someone to bounce ideas off of and to get pep talks from. For the most part, both of you will probably not have PMS on the same day, and you can encourage and remind each other of the end goals that you share. Ideally, you'll partner with someone who has a different skill set than yours. For one of my endeavors, my business partner is a computer whiz. She can read code like no one else, and she's really good at creating spreadsheets and getting tasks accomplished quickly. She refers to herself as a ninja squirrel, and she'll be the first to tell you she's not an extrovert (except digitally). We complement each other very well. I'm a big-picture thinker, and I love speaking to big crowds. She works behind the scenes to get the job done quickly and efficiently.

Check out CoFoundersLab.com to find a business partner that matches your DNA. I don't know if I would ever consider hooking up with a business partner I didn't know personally beforehand, but you never know. You might end up finding someone who gets your vision and has the resources to help take you where you want to go.

The Business Name

Check GoDaddy.com to view availability for the business name you'd like to operate under. If it's slim pickings for the name you'd like, you might want to rethink your business name. It's not imperative that you have a matching domain, but it does make things easier.

As soon as you've filed for a DBA and you've double-checked to make sure no one has secured the name with your state's secretary of state's office, go ahead and buy the domain name you've set your sights on. If you need to buy a few domain names that are similar, do so. You can always redirect the domain names to your main site. There's nothing worse than potential clients going to the wrong website because they made a slight error when typing your business name or there's another business that's very similar to yours in name. Hotels.com versus CheapHotels.com comes to mind here.

The EIN Number

An EIN is an exclusive nine-digit number the IRS assigns to businesses that operate in the US. It is also known as the Federal Employer Identification Number (FEIN). When used for identification versus tax reporting, it is usually referred to as a Taxpayer Identification Number (TIN). According to the IRS, the purpose of an EIN number is to help with tax administration. Most banks ask for it when you apply for a business account, and if you pay employees, you have to have one. Even if you don't have employees, an EIN is good to have.

Here are instructions on how to apply for and obtain an EIN: www.irs.gov/Businesses/Small-Businesses-&-Self-Employed/ Apply-for-an-Employer-Identification-Number-(EIN)-Online.

Taxes

As a business owner, one of your biggest headaches will be organizing your income and expenses and paying taxes. Just thinking about taxes gives me hives.

Here's a list of the likely taxes you'll need to pay:

» **Income tax or corporate tax.** Depending on whether you're a sole proprietor or a corporation, you'll have to report what your total business income is after expenses, and then you'll have to pay federal and state taxes on that income.

» **Self-employment tax.** On top of paying an income tax on your earnings, you may have to pay a self-employment tax that pays into social security and Medicare, which you would normally pay into if you were receiving a paycheck. If you have employees, you'll also have to pay their employment taxes in addition to FICA.

» **Sales tax.** If you ship or sell products to other people in your state, you must collect a tax for your state.

For me, reading up on tax law is worse than listening to someone scraping their fingernails down a chalkboard. Sometimes it's just a heck of a lot easier to pay a CPA to figure out all of the tax stuff for your business. But if you're totally bored and have nothing else to do, here's a link to the IRS Small Business and Self-Employed Tax Center: www.irs.gov/Businesses/Small-Businesses-&-Self-Employed. If you've taken one of the strengths tests I recommend and discovered you're very left brained and therefore actually like reading this stuff, maybe you can write a condensed version for the rest of us.

If you're selling anything that requires you to obtain sales tax, you need to get a sales tax license from your state. Most states charge a sales tax on goods sold within the state. This doesn't apply to selling some baby clothes on eBay, but it does apply if you sell stuff on eBay on a regular basis. At the time of publication, there's a little loophole though in that if you ship to someone out of state, you don't have to collect sales tax. That's right, you only have to collect sales tax if you sell to someone in your state.

Since your primary objective in 9-to-5 escape artist lifestyle design is to be able to work at locations other than your home, you probably won't have to collect sales tax all the time. You might have an e-commerce site, or you might be selling through auction sites or places like Etsy. Regardless of where you're selling your product, you'll only have to pay when it's shipped to someone in the same state as you. If you live in Oregon or Montana, then you're exempt because those states don't charge sales tax.

You'll want to implement some sort of order for your business when it comes to accounting and taxes. There's nothing worse than getting an audit notice and then not having the documents you need to help you out when you'll most need it. If you can get into the habit of taking a picture of your receipts, categorizing them properly, and accurately keeping track of your expenses, tax time will be a breeze.

Here's a list of a few apps that'll save you lots of time:

- » **IDonatedIt** www.idonatedit.com (Keeps track of your donations.)
- » **AskaCPA** https://itunes.apple.com/us/app/ ask-a-cpa-tax-answers-free/id503945103
- » **Doxo** www.doxo.com
- » **IXpenseIt** https://itunes.apple.com/us/app/ ixpenseit-expense-+-income/id284947174
- » **Spending Tracker** https://itunes.apple.com/us/app/ spending-tracker/id548615579
- » **OneReceipt** (Will scan Gmail or Yahoo mail for online receipts. If you're concerned about privacy, forward receipt emails to their supplied @onereceiptaddress and don't let them scan your emails.) www.onereceipt.com
- » **LifeLock Wallet** www.lifelock.com/services/mobile/
- » **Receipts by Wave** www.waveapps.com/receipts/

Chapter Eleven

POSITIONING YOUR BUSINESS

Call it a clan, call it a network, call it a tribe, call it a family.
Whatever you call it, whoever you are, you need one.
—JANE HOWARD

Positioning in regard to your business simply means how your business fits within your market niche and how you want customers to define what it is that you do. Don't get too caught up in planning for positioning. You should have a strategic plan, but don't get stuck in the brainstorming stage. Implementation should be your prime objective. Just get out of your head and do it. Sometimes you just need to hit the pavement (or the keyboard, depending on what your business is) and get moving. The quickest way to see what works and what doesn't work is to take action and review the results afterwards.

Find a niche and rock it. Listen to your customers or buyers. If they like what you're selling, then keep selling it. If they hate it, then kill it.

If you don't develop a tribe of influencers for your business, it's going to be a lot harder to get your message out into the world.

Social media is great and all, but think about how much easier spreading messages can be when more than one person is talking.

The key to developing a tribe of people who'll spread your message is to identify those who are passionate about you, your company, or your product, *and* they're willing and excited to talk to others about you. I call these people *influencers*, aka VIPs.

When you're getting ready to launch a new business, feel people out. Not in a creepy, manipulative way. Simply ask yourself, "In my sphere, who are the leaders and influencers?"

> *...social media influencers aren't the alternatives to celebrities; they are the new celebrities.*

Influencers are not necessarily the loudest people on social media; they're the ones who can propel others to go or do or buy something solely on their recommendations. Their followers are people who trust them, and they'll in turn go and do what they say.

Next to word-of-mouth referrals, amplification via social media is the quickest conversion to recognition and sales for your product or service. There's no better way to do this than by having a social media influencer in your tribe. It's noteworthy that social media influencers aren't the alternatives to celebrities; they *are* the new celebrities. According to Variety Survey, US teenagers are more enamored with YouTube stars than they are the biggest celebrities in film, TV, and music.

Examples of 2015 influencers today are Guy Kawasaki, Arianna Huffington, Mark Zuckerberg, the Kardashians, and supposedly Justin Bieber and Miley Cyrus for the teens (heaven help us). The former have built large platforms with a devoted following. The latter are influencers because they're sort of bad. They break rules and turn heads. I'm not sure we want those kinds of influencers talking about our business(es), but you should always consider all options at your disposal.

Fans trust influencers and are inspired by them. Influencers usually leverage many different social media platforms and can direct large waves of traffic to your blog or website. They're also trendsetters. If you have a cutting-edge idea or product, pitch it to an influencer. Influencers are usually also connectors in that if they can't help you attain your goals, they usually know someone in their sphere who can.

What does this practically look like? Influencers share. If they're excited about your product or wowed by your service, they'll write a blog post, tweet about you, or give you an endorsement. Before you launch your business idea, contact these influencers and give them details. Let them know all about what you're doing in a clear and concise way. Give them actionable items to perform for you and reward them with giving them your undying devotion or your first-born.

The first step is to create an email campaign using MailChimp. com to alert those people whom you believe will want to contribute to your success. Hopefully some of them will actively help you out by spreading the message about your service or product. Make the email subject line catchy. Implore the recipient to take action and give them a way to do so. Use a clickable button to take them where they need to go. Once they land on the page you want them to, make it easy for them to do what you want them to. If you give people too many choices, they'll get frustrated and not do anything. You've heard it before: KIS or Keep It Simple (you're not stupid because you're a 9-to-5 escape artist, so I'm omitting the last S that customarily goes there).

I had a friend who launched an amazing book about all of the great places to eat in our state. She'd spent the last few years visiting hole-in-the-wall and unknown but awesome places to eat. With rich description and calls to adventure in food discovery, she had a great concept. Before the book launch, she created a tribe of people, including me, and asked us if she could put us all together in a Facebook group with the sole intent to give us all updates about her book.

I thought it was a great idea and wanted to contribute to her success. She did great but could've done more. What about asking all of us for a fair review on Amazon in exchange for a free digital copy? With no out-of-pocket expense to her, she could've secured lots of reviews from those who cared about the success of the book. What about asking all of us if we could recommend one retailer to her who might consider carrying her book in their store? Out of forty people in the influencers group, she'd most certainly connect with a few key retailers in our area, helping to increase her visibility.

Sometimes all you need to do is just ask. People can say no, but if you make your request an easy one, you'll probably get a yes. And don't give up the first time. I know it seems counterintuitive, but if you don't get a response, ask a few times. Sometimes emails get buried and distractions keep us from responding to requests we'd like to take action upon. A simple "did you get my email" won't annoy anyone.

If you use an email program like MailChimp, you can track who opens up your email request. This is infinitely helpful when you want to see who's read your requests. If MailChimp shows the person didn't even click, then your email might've gone to spam. Never assume someone is ignoring you if they don't respond to your request.

Exchanging a good or service for a public recommendation can be very effective. If you design websites, you could offer to design a landing page for an influencer or help them fix a problem on their site that no one else has been able to fix. If you offer virtual assistant services, you could contact an influencer in your sphere and ask them if you can schedule their social media posts within Hootsuite for a few days for free. If you're a freelance editor, maybe offer to review the first ten pages of someone's manuscript in progress. Don't you think that person will happily tell others about your service?

Influencers take their role seriously and won't shout from the rooftops about your product unless you let them know why they should. Spend time crafting your pitch and make sure you're launching a visually appealing website that's easy to navigate. Influencers are always proud to be the first to know about new businesses. It really strokes their (balanced) egos.

Influencers aren't always on social media, but in the digital age we live in, you want to target those who are. Don't leave out the ones who aren't though. You want to have as much exposure as you can. Non-social media influencers might be heads of large networking or niche groups. Make sure to send them an actionable email request and a press release so you're keeping them in the know.

$mart Tip: Identify the influencers in your sphere and set social media alerts on them. This will help you stay informed about what they have going on in their important endeavors. Influencers love reciprocity, and if you stay connected to their requests, they'll make it a priority to help you out too.

Chapter Twelve

KICK-ASS MARKETING STRATEGIES

So, you've identified your business product(s) or service and have implemented the necessary foundations in order to be able to sell. Your website is spiffy, and your business is now ready to receive real dollars because you've set up the payment processing and billing systems. You're legal with an officially filed business name and appropriate licenses. Now all you need are people to buy whatever it is you're selling.

In my humble opinion, traditional marketing is dead. In fact, it's been dead for quite a while, so there's no use in beating the (very) dead horse. When was the last time you didn't fast-forward through the commercials of your favorite pre-recorded TV show? Do you remember when you actually spent time looking through all of the mailers you received in your mailbox, carefully reading all of the fine print and bullet points?

Yet there are still those who insist on following traditional marketing methods because that's what people were taught in college ten years ago—and maybe even today. I still think some professors at the college level are teaching what they know has worked in the past, not necessarily what's trending now. After all, if you're not in the trenches, it's hard to stay abreast of the battle strategies.

Those who are in the traditional camp are the ones spending thousands of dollars on a paper phone book ad. I cringe every six months when a six-inch-thick, yellow-paged book is dropped on my doorstep, and I do what most of you probably do. I try to throw it back at the head of the person who threw it into my flowerbed. After missing their head, I briefly consider how many trees were killed in the process of making the useless book, and I walk the blasted creation over to the side of my house and dump it in the recycle bin. Refuse collectors must wonder why once every six months the bins are exceptionally heavy.

Google is the new phone book, and it's been that way for a long time. Everyone has a smartphone. To my knowledge, Siri doesn't scan the phone book, but she does connect with Google when I'm asking her where the nearest coffee shop is. If you really want to spend a thousand dollars, why not spend a thousand dollars on Google ads instead of the book that no one looks at?

Just like Dr. Seuss's *The Lorax*, I implore you on behalf of the trees to quit wasting paper products on your marketing efforts. We live in the digital age. That means no paper exchange is necessary. Everything you do can be done within the digital realm, even obtaining binding signatures (check out Docusign.net).

Marketing is identifying and determining one or more distribution channels to reach customers or clients. A **marketing strategy** combines all of your goals into one cohesive and workable plan. It will help you implement the way you're going to develop a demand for your product or service. In our fast-moving digital society, a marketing strategy includes building your platform.

According to retired Harvard Business School Professor of Marketing Theodore C. Levitt, marketing "views the entire business process as consisting of a tightly integrated effort to discover, create, arouse and satisfy customer needs."

A **marketing plan** is the way you're going to tell people about you or your product and get them to actually buy it.

You'll find many templates and ideas on how to write a marketing plan by visiting Slideshare.net and typing *marketing plan* in the search bar.

Integrate Google analytics into your marketing plan (see chapter 18 on Metrics). You need to have analytics to help you understand how people are finding you and if they convert into a sale once they do. You'll also want to do some keyword research when you're outlining your marketing plan. You need to know what words your target market is typing into the search bar. Here's a quick YouTube video to teach you how to use Google Keyword planner: www.youtube.com/watch?v=3kFooXfo58M.

Keep your marketing plan close to you. Always adhere to the basic outline of the plan so nothing falls through the cracks. Every piece of your plan needs to fit together like a well-thought-out puzzle. Your marketing plan can constantly change, and keeping it updated will ensure your business stays on track with your goals. Review your plan often, and adjust it whenever you learn something new about your customers or when you learn about a new actionable marketing tactic.

$mart Tip: If you're like me and have a million ideas rolling around in your head, make sure you immediately capture each one. Speak your idea into your smartphone or create a list using the Wunderlist app and title the list: Marketing Ideas. Check the list often and implement at least one new idea every week.

The Basics of Social Media

I'm admittedly a social media junkie. I was on social media sites when most people thought social media meant TV ads pertaining to partying.

I invited everyone I knew to join Facebook in 2007, and most of them thought I was asking them to join a site like Shutterfly so they could look at my family pictures. When they started to join in late 2008 and early 2009, my circle said, "Why didn't you tell me how fun this was?" (Sigh.)

When I invited my sphere to join Pinterest, they replied, "Who has the time to look at pictures all day?" and I was informed by well-meaning colleagues (ahem, mostly men) that only bored and broke stay-at-home moms did stuff like that and there was no conversion practicality there. Now Pinterest has 70 million users and growing. Thirty-eight percent of all active users bought something because they saw it on Pinterest, and forty-three percent of them were moms[5]. Smart people understand that men may try to wear the pants in a family, but we women are the ones who bought those pants after seeing a hot guy wear them on Pinterest. Don't ever discredit the correlation between SAHMs (stay-at-home moms) and purchasing power!

Right now, the majority of social media users are still on Facebook and Twitter. LinkedIn and YouTube are neck and neck, and Pinterest and Google+ are growing steadily. Fewer people are on Instagram, but don't discredit it. Beautiful, personalized picture advertising taps into different areas of the brain than reading highly specialized blog content. Instagram still doesn't have

---

5 Source: www.adweek.com/news/advertising-branding/
pinterest-users-dont-mind-ads-point-157944

clickable links in posts, so you have to strategically direct potential customers.

Social media removes all barriers to reaching your audience. *Everyone* is on social media, except maybe conspiracy theory advocates and those on life support. Even my ninety-year-old grandma is on Facebook. Social media levels the playing field and opens up unlimited opportunities to reach the previously unreachable. Small business startups can compete with bigger players, equaling the playing field.

Used correctly, social media can help you build your brand, increase your platform or following, and connect you with your customers or clients in a way that couldn't be accomplished before. Here's the caveat: you have to use it correctly. You have to know each platform you're using and how to use it. "Likes" or "followers" are important for social credibility but not as important as whether or not you're converting these into sales. Meaning you're receiving actual dollars in exchange for your marketing efforts.

There are lots of books about social marketing that I've listed in the back of this book. In all of your spare time, you can read all twenty of them. In the meantime, I'm going to touch on each relevant main social network and give you some tips and tricks to utilize for the purpose of marketing your business.

The way you speak to your audience and how you present information will vary depending on which social media platform you are posting to. For instance, if you're a soap maker and you post on Twitter, you'd tweet, "I'm making #soap." On YouTube, you'd make a video titled, "Here I Am Making Soap." On LinkedIn, you'd list that your skills include soap making. On Instagram, you'd post a picture with the caption, "Here is my soap." And on Pinterest, your post would be, "Here's my soap recipe." Same message but different ways to deliver the message.

The most important aspects of using social media are to be socially kind and to post relevant and informational content. Always remember to use your social media platform to give value to your audience, which will in turn convert into sales. Don't ever engage with trolls (people having a really bad day or those who were born with a bad attitude and just like to stir the pot). Always thank people for their feedback no matter what that feedback is and remember not to engage in social media warfare.

Hootsuite

Use Hootsuite.com to schedule your social media marketing posts. You can use one service to manage all of your social media sites at the same time. One of the biggest reasons most people don't use social media effectively is because they just don't have the time. Hootsuite brings in most of your social media streams, giving you the capability to view, comment, and pre-schedule updates. If you batch your time and spend an hour scheduling posts for the future, it'll appear to your clients or customers that you're very active on social media. It's helpful to use an Excel spreadsheet scheduling calendar to keep track of your posts so you can determine what posts may have generated more sales or followers. Hootsuite is free for up to three social media accounts, and a mobile app is available for ease of use on the go.

Hashtag

Identify what you are talking about and how you can be found by using the hashtag (#) symbol after your text. Capitalize the first letter of each word so the reader can quickly assimilate the information without having to read it again. For example, #SocialMediaTips is much easier to visually digest than #socialmediatips.

Best Time to Post

There's a lot of advice on the web regarding what the best time(s) to post on social media are. The information varies based on who is conducting the research, but it's safe to say there are certain days and times that are more effective than others to schedule your posts. More people are on Facebook on Thursdays and Fridays, and posting around 1 p.m. will yield the most shares. You will get more engagement from Twitter users Monday through Friday, and 5 p.m. is suggested for the highest retweets. According to LinkedIn, posting during weekdays through the course of the business day is best. The best day to post on Pinterest is Saturday from 8 p.m. to 11 p.m. and 2 a.m. to 4 a.m. (it looks likes women would rather be on Pinterest than sleep). Google+ users are highly engaged on Wednesdays at 9 a.m. and prefer to utilize Google+ mostly on weekdays later in the morning.[6]

Be Aware of Your Customer Service

Social media is an amplifier, for better or worse. If you've competitively priced your product and have placed yourself equally with your top competitors, one of the main factors that will set you apart from them is customer service. A customer might be willing to pay a little more for your product or service if you set yourself apart and offer your customer an amazing experience.

Alternatively, if you provide poor customer service and support, everyone is going to hear about it because now it's easy and free to socially bash a company. I admit when I have an amazing experience with an online retailer or service provider, I'm going to tell everyone in my network about it. Rarely have I disparaged someone or something,

6 Source: www.adweek.com/socialtimes/best-time-to-post-social-media/504222

with the exception of the salon that ruined my daughter's hair and wouldn't fix it. When a company listens to customers and applies their feedback, they're creating a company edge.

Purposeful Marketing

Sometimes you have to throw crap at the wall to see what sticks. Sometimes you'll be totally surprised at what works and what doesn't, but you should be strategic about your marketing. You need to schedule your marketing with purposeful intent and measure the results. If you don't have a strategy for your marketing, then you'll have a hard time measuring the results. It's okay to want to have five hundred likes on your Facebook page, but if you have no way of measuring if those likes are converting into a sale, then what's the point?

Purposeful marketing is identifying exactly what your intent is and how you'll measure the success of the marketing endeavor. Your marketing plan will have identifiable objectives and measurable results.

For instance:
» By x date I want to have x paying customers.
» By x date I want to have x people on my email list.
» By x date I want to have x people on my Facebook page with x% interacting daily with me.

Interestingly, a 2012 study by Edelman called the Goodpurpose Study cites that when quality and price are the same, social purpose is the most important factor.[7] Only 28 percent of consumers

---

7 Source: www.slideshare.net/EdelmanInsights/
global-deck-2012-edelman-goodpurpose-study/1

believed businesses are performing well in addressing societal issues. Fifty-five percent believed CEOs should publicly support societal issues. Fifty-one percent believed companies should donate a portion of profits to a cause.

Hitting people over the head with your product or services is not the key. Leading with purposeful intent is the key to marketing correctly. If you're selling something, the wrong way to market is to constantly ask someone to buy it. For instance, if you're selling shoes and post on Twitter, *Buy our shoes!* and then you're posting again a few minutes later—*Our shoes are awesome, get yours today!*— then people will completely dismiss your pleas because you're annoying. But if you say, *Buy our shoes and we'll donate another pair,* or, *One for One* (The slogan for TOMS™ shoes), people will buy the shoes. Consumers are more likely to follow a brand if it has a strong purpose in doing something for society's betterment. Don't be selfish and try to lambast others with all-about-you marketing. Nobody likes to hang around someone who only talks about themselves at a party. Put your customers first and figure out what they want to see from you and what they need to hear from you. Then do it.

Blogging

As of 2015, most everyone has heard of the term blogging, but only a very small percentage of small businesses are actively blogging. Blogging increases credibility and can give your audience social proof that you know what you're talking about. Blogging is very helpful in ranking your business within Google, and if you utilize tags within your posts, you're helping with search engine optimization.

Using the **BuzzSumo** app (BuzzSumo.com), you can easily see what's trending online and create content for your blog based on what's trending. You don't have to be an amazing writer; just make sure you have a main point, a great middle, and a call-to-action wrap up. No one is going to be as critical about your blog posts as you are, so don't get caught up in perfectionism. It's way better to be a mediocre blogger with content than to be a business owner who doesn't blog at all.

Using a title generator is a fun and easy way to spark creativity when you're stuck in a writing rut. There are a few tools to help you come up with some great titles. For example, my daughter has Autism, and if I wanted to create a blog post about Autism using Portent's title maker, the title generated after inputting Autism into the subject line is: "How Autism is the Answer to Middle East Peace." Now that's a unique title!

Tweak Your Biz's website came up with over seventy blog post titles using the subject Autism, of which my favorite was: "Fighting for Autism: The Samurai Way." With these tools, there's really no excuse for not coming up with great blog post titles, which will in turn prompt you to come up with some unique blog posts. Some of the generated titles might be too off-the-wall to use, but at least you'll get lots of ideas for a distinct title.

Check these blog title tools out:
- » www.backlinkgenerator.net/titlegenerator
- » http://portent.com/tools/title-maker
- » http://tweakyourbiz.com/tools/title-generator/

Guest blogging on other websites can be a great way to grow your following. Consider approaching other businesses that might benefit from your writing and expertise. Usually other bloggers are happy to have a guest post from someone else. If you write a great post, some readers will look you up on your social media sites and follow you. They might even visit your website, and you can capture their email address for future contact.

Even the writing pros make mistakes, so it's important to check your work. If you don't have someone on staff to edit your blog posts, you can use free tools like ProWritingAid.com or Grammarly.com. These websites are a quick and easy way to help you strengthen your writing. You can upgrade to the pro accounts for a fee.

The secret to creating viral blog posts is to look at your target audience. They are either bored at work or bored online. Use incredibly strong emotional triggers within your blog titles and blog text.

Steps:
- » Begin with the reward (8 ideas ...)
- » Or begin with enticing keywords (Free ... Contest)
- » Or speak directly to the reader (You can ...)

Remember:
- » Be timely (create a post after a headline, debate, etc.)
- » Provide a call to action and/or a way for your readers to reach you (a link to your website, your social media sites, your email, etc.)
- » Make your statements concise with a minimum blog post word count of 900 words and maximum word count of 1600 words

Blogging is a free way to increase your reach. If you don't like to write, visit content sites like Textbroker.com or WritersAccess.com to connect with writers who can create great content for you. Your blog is the online face of your company. Don't you want to look like you know what you're talking about?

Share you blog posts everywhere. Shrink the web link using Bitly.com and then share your content to *all* of the social networks. Always make sure to check Bitly to track how many opens you're getting and where you're getting them.

$mart Tip: Submit your blog to the following blog directories:
  » Blogarama.com
  » BlogCatalog.com
  » BlogFlux.com
  » BlogHer.com
  » BlogHub.com
  » GlobeofBlogs.com

Twitter

When Twitter started, most of my friends thought the concept of typing messages limited to 140 characters was ridiculous, and no one "got" what I was trying to convey. I was okay with this because I wasn't on Twitter to connect with my friends. When used appropriately, Twitter can enlarge your audience locally and internationally. You can connect with people you never would've been able to talk to before the existence of social media. But most people use Twitter incorrectly and completely miss the point of relationship building and effective Tweets.

A TWITTER HORROR STORY

All of the teenagers are on Twitter (and Snapchat). Facebook isn't their preference currently because all of us parents are on Facebook. Twitter is fast-paced, most parents aren't monitoring it yet, and it's real-time with notifications (using the @ symbol to tag someone and communicate).

My teen is on the competitive cheer team at her high school. We do a hybrid homeschooling program so that my kids can do extra-curricular activities at our local schools and tackle the core courses at home or on the road so we can have flexibility for our lifestyle designs.

One night my daughter was at a sleepover with other girls from her school. A naughty (or vindictive) teenager took a picture of my daughter bending over in short shorts. The bratty teen who shall remain nameless even though I wanted to strangle her posted the picture to her Twitter account with a caption like "Check out this slut" or something like that.

The tweet went viral, and everyone at my daughter's school, including the principal and the cheer coach, saw it. Her butt cheek was sort of hanging out of her shorts, so the picture was slightly pornographic. The worst part was that the shorts had the name of the high school on them. They're school issued, and she wears them underneath her cheer uniform.

My daughter started getting texts while at the sleepover about the picture, and you can bet I called the police to go visit that girl's mom (she can be tried as an accomplice to child pornography). Immediately upon hearing about it, the reigning mom at the sleepover made the super-evil child who posted the picture remove the tweet, but it was too late. Everyone had already seen it, and a few had taken screenshots of it for later viewing pleasure or for blackmail.

My girl was suspended from the cheer team for one week and wasn't able to participate in the first assembly of the school year. Not to mention, she was publicly humiliated. I certainly did my best to plead her case and almost ended up holding a sign outside of the school district building. The girl who took the picture didn't get suspended or receive any formal reprimand.

So why am I sharing this with you? For a few reasons. To tell you to watch out for your kid on social media. Just because you have access to their account doesn't mean you're catching everything that's happening. Secondly, I want to show you that you can be a victim of social media if you accidentally or intentionally bend over and show your stuff. Be mindful of what you are posting and what others are posting about you. Keep an eye out for social media trolls, those who'd like to take you down or go against you with the purpose of smearing you or your message. Don't give anyone an opportunity to discredit you or your business or tarnish your reputation.

LISTS

Twitter is a totally different animal than Facebook, and herein lies the problem. You can't possibly keep up with all of the total strangers who will start following you, and Twitter is completely hit and miss. Unless you set it up properly. The key is to make sure that when you follow someone that you truly want to keep up with, you put them in a **list**.

Lists can be public or private, and you can organize all of your followers and all of the people that you follow in a list. I have a list consisting of close friends, fellow writers, marketing gurus, and even a list of my favorite local restaurants. When I want to get updates on what's trending in marketing, I quickly look at tweets from people in my marketing list or type in #MarketingTips. If I want to see if there are any specials happening at my favorite watering holes, I can see those tweets in a matter of seconds.

Finding people with common interests is easy. Just use the hashtag (#) to identify people who may be fun to follow. For instance, I like #entrepreneurs, #speakers, #writers, etc.

DIRECT MESSAGES

You can block spammers who send you stupid Direct Messages (DMs) by clicking on the User Actions tab and clicking "Block User." And don't direct message someone unless you're asking a personalized question. I hardly ever check my direct messages because they're always so spammy.

Don't spam new followers with a DM. Send them a personal public tweet instead. I never click any links that new followers or people I have chosen to follow send me via DM because if I did that, I'd be on Twitter all day long. Use the DM sparingly. If you want to tell someone they have an email from you, or if you want to meet up with someone, then this would be a great use of the direct message feature within Twitter.

BUILDING A PLATFORM

I have realized that although Twitter may differentiate itself from Facebook in that total strangers can see your posts, it actually opens up unlimited opportunity to randomly connect with anyone in the world. I just had a conversation with an author from Israel via Twitter. I also had a follower send me a link to a classic car for sale on eBay after I posted a picture of a hot rod I loved but didn't know the make or model of. I have also converted followers into clients by just being friendly on Twitter.

It's important to weed the spammers out of your stream, and this includes the uber-annoying tweeps who follow people and then un-follow them the next day. (If you haven't guessed, a tweep is just another name for a Twitter user.) I love the free tools that tell you who follows you and then whether they un-follow you or not. You can then return the favor. Visit Manageflitter and Justunfollow to get this accomplished for free.

Remember that the whole point of this social media marketing thing is that you are trying to build a platform and an audience. If you don't spam people (Buy my book! Buy my product!) and if you provide engaging and entertaining content, Twitter will eventually pay off for you. And don't pay someone to get you 100k followers. That doesn't work because fake followers won't engage with you and spread your message.

With Twitter, you should spend some time on your bio. This is your one shot to convert someone into a sale or future client. Use a specialized web link from Twitter to your website. For example, YourWebsite.com/twitter and customize this web page to your Twitter followers. Say something like, "Welcome, Twitter followers! Here's how to navigate my site" (and then direct them to what you'd like them to do).

Pictures grab attention faster than posts, so add rich media to your tweets. Here's how to do it: https://dev.twitter.com/docs/cards.

You'll also want to familiarize yourself with Twitter's advanced search tool to help you refine searches for trends and followers: https://twitter.com/search-advanced. Keep up to date with Twitter trends on the Twitter small business blog: https://blog.twitter.com/small-business.

Start here for a business account: http://business.twitter.com.

Twitter designed their platform with a 2000/10 percent rule for followers. Once you've followed 2000 other users, Twitter limits how many more users you can follow based on a ratio of how many people follow you to how many people you are following. Read this for more information: https://support.twitter.com/articles/68916-following-rules-and-best-practices. And read this for information on how to break through these barriers: http://

marketingtips4authors.blogspot.com/2013/02/understanding-twitters-200010-rule.html.

There are a few great apps for your smartphone that will allow you to easily add a screenshot to your tweet and can extract images from links you post on Twitter. (Twitshot is currently my favorite mobile app for Twitter media posting while I'm out and about.) Ask any teenager: Twitter is the new Facebook. If the upcoming buying generation is on Twitter, then you're going to have to be on Twitter too.

StumbleUpon

StumbleUpon (StumbleUpon.com) is a social media discovery tool customized to a user's personal interests. The user identifies interests when the account is set up, and StumbleUpon learns as the user stumbles upon new information. It can be used as a powerful tool to drive traffic to your website or blog, as it's a great way for users to discover you when they wouldn't have done so had they not been presented with your information.

New users are asked for their interests once a profile has been created, and these initial choices will determine what content StumbleUpon shows you. A user can change interests at any time. Not only can users like a page, they can also put pages into lists. This helps credibility and discoverability. Users can also share a page that they've liked to other social media networks.

Highly liked Stumbles will show up in the trending sections. You can also see comments on pages you like (and your pages), and you can follow up to five hundred other StumbleUpon users.

StumbleUpon's biggest competition is Pinterest, but you shouldn't set it aside. Different users are on Pinterest for different reasons. I personally like StumbleUpon for the randomness of it. There's something intensely satisfying about being presented with information from a website that you've never seen before and would've never seen had you not Stumbled it.

A tip: the search button doesn't let you search site-wide. Instead, text you enter in the search bar only searches the category and subcategory you're on. For example, if you're trying to search for a StumbleUpon user, you must be in the Follow > Stumblers tab. If you're in Follow > Lists, you won't find what you were looking for.

Create lists within StumbleUpon and fill them with great content. Mix your content in here and there. You'll get new followers, and your content will be interspersed for more views. Give StumbleUpon a try. It's really fun to stumble upon new content you've never seen before. It's also especially useful when you're trying to fall asleep and you want something to do but just don't want to read any more blogs or dive into a book.

For more information, here's a comprehensive user guide: http://help.stumbleupon.com/customer/portal/articles/665195-new-user-guide.

Instagram

Instagram is a newer social media platform specific to sharing photos that users can apply digital filters to. The name is a combination of the words instant (cameras) and telegram. It's visually stimulating and mostly ad-free. The benefit of joining now is that not everyone has caught onto it yet. Facebook bought it for $750 million, so obviously those developers at Facebook see the value in it. Anytime Mark Zuckerberg forges ahead, it's best if we small business owners and 9-to-5 escape artists just follow along in allegiance. His tide is way too big to ignore. Actually, he's more like a tsunami.

Instagram use has doubled in social media users from 15 percent in 2012 to 32 percent in 2014, with 300 million active users. Unlike other social media platforms, Instagram is almost entirely mobile based. You can only use the web platform to view posts. Picture and video uploads and picture customization only work on mobile. As of this printing, there's no way to specify a business account versus a personal account. Because I have teens, I know almost all teenagers are on Instagram, a good indicator this platform is on trend.

At the moment, bloggers, artists, and product-based businesses do best on Instagram. Currently, Instagram doesn't allow you to post a web link in the comments section of your post, so you always need to refer back to a link within your main profile. The trick to Instagram is to share organic pictures, or pictures you've actually taken. For great ideas, check out Starbucks' Instagram page. With 3.8 million followers, they're obviously doing something right.

Unlike Facebook, you're only sharing your own pictures. Users aren't retiring or reposting articles and text content in the same way they are on Facebook. Sharing pictures from other users is possible, but only do this sporadically and make sure you mention the user whom you lifted a picture from, using the @ sign and their username (otherwise known as attribution). The Regram.me app can be used to re-post other Instagram users' pictures as well as the **Repost Whiz** app (available on iTunes).

For Instagram analytics, you can use Inconsquare.com. You'll just need to link Instagram to it, and it'll provide insights into your followers, what your most popular pictures are, and other information you may or may not find useful. I like the extra tools, like the Facebook header generator that takes your recent pictures and scrambles them in a fun banner for your Facebook personal or fan page.

Play around with Instagram and see what happens. You may find it's the perfect fit for your business. Build your audience by tagging others in your photos and mentioning others (by typing the @ symbol, followed by the person's username). When you want to reply to a comment, you need to follow the same procedure so that the person receives a notification.

Use hashtags (#) to identify your topic, brand, or product. This is a great way for new users to find you, and it can increase your followers. You're also able to geotag your pictures, so if you're so inclined, you can add a location to your pictures (similar to a check-in on Facebook).

A few ways to use Instagram for marketing purposes would be to ask your customers or clients to post pictures of your business or brand using a predetermined hashtag. For instance, if you are a graphic artist and you just created some great business cards, ask your client to post a picture of them on their Instagram page, mentioning you (@username) and using a hashtag you choose (#AmazingBusinessCardDesign).

If you have employees, ask them to share pictures of themselves at work or working on your product. It's also fun to post behind-the-scenes pictures, especially if you are creating something or enjoying a unique experience. You can also run contests and give-aways by asking your audience to share an image in order to be entered into a drawing. You can also increase followers by asking them to follow you after they've just done a business transaction with you.

Just like Pinterest, Instagram has a specific appeal to those who love to be visually entertained. It's easy on the mind to look at pictures instead of a whole bunch of text. The brain can easily absorb a lovely picture, and it's a quick and easy way to reach people. If you're not active on Instagram, give it a try. You might be pleasantly surprised that your marketing is fun again.

Here are some great apps to enhance your Instagram experience:

» **Videohance** (Edits videos for Instagram. **VideoShow** is the android version.)
» **IWatermark** (Put your logo or name on your photos.)
» **Flipagram** (Create a video using your pictures.)
» **Diptic** (Scrapbook layouts for your photos.)
» **Emoji** (Add symbols like smiley faces to your pictures.)
» **Word Swag** (Add text to your images. **A Beautiful Mess** is an android alternative.)
» **Instasize** (Resize your photo to fit Instagram's specifications.)

$mart Tip: Use an app like InsTrack by Innovatty, LLC to see who un-followed you, who blocked you, and who isn't following you back.

Facebook

It's *really* hard to ensure your fan page posts will be shown to your audience unless you're paying to boost your posts. Not to say you shouldn't keep trying, but don't put all of your eggs in the Facebook basket. Regularly share relevant content and make an attempt to connect with your audience.

Facebook is like jail; you sit around and waste time, write on walls, and get poked by people you don't know.
—VERYBESTQUOTES.COM

I don't need to spend a lot of time explaining Facebook because most of you are already using it. I have a personal page and a few business pages. Sometimes I share content from my business pages to my personal page and vice versa. For now, this tactic seems to be boosting my shares, likes, and views. You have to keep trying new things on Facebook, and once you figure out what works, they'll probably change their algorithms. They like to keep us guessing.

You can embed an HTML sign-up form tab for MailChimp on your Facebook fan page so you can alert clients about things that are going on. You can also create HTML tabs for contests, coupons, etc. Custom tabs can be created using any of the following apps:

» Heyo
» Tabfoundry
» ShortStack
» Pagemodo
» Tabsite
» Static HTML – Thunderpenny
» LeadPages
» Woobox
» Wishpond
» Canva.com is my favorite way to create the custom 120 x 120 image tabs. Using their drag and drop system, you'll have custom images within a few minutes. Canva can also be used to create Facebook banners.

Make sure you're using the business analytics tools for metrics so you can see which posts are popular, when the best time for you to post might be, and what your weekly and monthly history is. Always make sure when you share a link on your Facebook page you shrink it first using Bitly.com. This will ensure true analytics and give you insight into more than just views, including whether or not your audience is clicking through the links you're sharing.

Try using the fun features of Facebook to keep your audience engaged. Apps like **LiveStream** (https://apps.facebook.com/livestream/) allow you to host a live event on your Facebook page—for a fee. Rafflecopter.com is a fun way to host contests and giveaways, and their $9-a-month fee is worth it because you can use it within emails and it integrates with other social media networks.

Keep working Facebook because everyone expects you to have a Facebook presence, but don't spend hours on it. I'm getting tired of it, and so are a lot of people. It's completely hit and miss now, and there might be better platforms out there to focus your time and attention on.

Of course you can spend money to boost your posts and spend money trying to get new likes, but will those likes really convert into sales? Use the analytics tools to make sure you're using Facebook appropriately. Stay on top of changes by reading the Facebook for business blog: www.facebook.com/business/news/.

> $mart Tip: Use **LikeAlyzer** to check your Facebook page statistics. It'll give you suggestions for modifying your Facebook posts to get maximum success.

Pinterest

Pinterest has been touted as a visual storyboard. Users create digital bulletin boards and save and display content they like (called pinning). Currently, 80 percent of the pictures on Pinterest are not unique but re-circulated content. This is great news for you if you're able to create content on your blog or website and pin it to Pinterest. By creating new and unique content, you'll keep your followers excited and wanting more.

Most of the 71 million users on Pinterest are women, so if you're trying to get new customers for your male enhancement products, you'll want to post a picture of a beautiful and happy woman on Pinterest. The few male Pinterest users will be interested, and the female users might consider clicking through to your blog if you have a catchy tagline under the pin or text across the picture.

When signing up for Pinterest, it's important to make sure you create a business account versus an individual account, which is the automatic choice. Business accounts will give you extra tools, like analytics to measure how well you're doing on Pinterest. Visit http://business.pinterest.com to learn about business accounts. When you set up your boards on Pinterest, make sure they are in alignment with your business or brand.

If you're a fitness coach, you're going to want to create boards pertinent to your clientele. You may consider creating boards such as health tips, healthy recipes, ways to de-stress, and other similar topics. You'll want to intersperse content from your personal blog by pinning your content to one of the boards you've created.

When creating new content on your website, it's important that you embed a pin-it button under all of your posts. You can accomplish this on whatever platform you're using by adding a Pinterest widget to your website. This will enable you to easily share from your website directly to Pinterest (in the form of creating a new pin) as well as allowing others to easily share your content. There are many applications you can install on your website that will allow readers to pin your web content directly to Pinterest. If you're using a WordPress template, you can install a number of Pinterest plugins. Simply type in the word Pinterest within the widgets search bar and you'll be given quite a few plugin options.

Similar to the other social media networks, you'll identify your pins as topics using the hashtag (#). This way, your topic will come up in search results. Just like Twitter, you can tag other users using the @ symbol and then the username of the person you'd like to tag. They will then receive a notification that you've tagged them. When you tag other users while commenting or liking pins, you're building your brand by engaging with the Pinterest community.

Make sure you connect Pinterest to as many other social accounts as possible to find users within your sphere. Connecting to your Gmail or Yahoo account will allow you to easily connect with people you already engage with who are on Pinterest. You can then invite them to follow you on Pinterest.

Advanced users should consider using rich pins, pins that include extra information right on the pin itself. If you're a food blogger or have a product or app to sell, you'd be missing out if you didn't apply for rich pin use. Visit https://business.pinterest.com/en/rich-pins for details. First consider which type of rich pin best suits you and add the metatags to your website. Then you must validate your rich pin and apply for them to be uploaded to Pinterest.

If you'd like to use a program that allows you to schedule pins and easily monitor Pinterest, try TailWindApp.com. They offer a free trial so you can play around with the many helpful business management tools for Pinterest. You can calendar out your pins, determine when your audience is the most engaged, and ultimately you'll save a lot of time. If you decide to sign up for their service, monthly plans start at around $10. If you are spending the bulk of your marketing time on Pinterest, a small investment in TailWind will save you a lot of time.

Pinterest users are a huge market, especially if you have an artistic-type businesses, if you're a blogger, or if you have a product you'd like to get in front of people (especially women). Set up Pinterest properly, use rich pins, and engage with your community. Measure your results using the TailWind app. If you're like me, you'll have to set a timer for usage because you'll have so much fun on Pinterest the day might get away from you. Used correctly, Pinterest has great potential to turn a Pinterest user into a paying customer.

Pandora

Pandora is a music-streaming site, customizable to your tastes. Currently, Pandora is the largest online radio source, representing

68 percent of all online radio listening and 8 percent of all radio listening. With 80 million active users a month, Pandora is prime for offering advertising benefits. New cars are even offering Pandora, and currently 5 million cars are outfitted to stream Pandora.

When new Pandora users sign up, they're required to give their gender and age. Combined with Pandora's unique music analysis system to profile listeners, advertisers have an advantage over standard broadcast radio. You can target your ads to certain geographic locations and by the music your target market listens to. You can also purchase clickable banner ads that customers can click on after you state your call to action.

After creating a profile, you choose favorite artists or tracks, and you can create stations and playlists. If Pandora plays a song you don't like, you simply click the thumbs-down icon, and Pandora won't play that song anymore. Most everyone I know uses the free version. You can upgrade to the paid version and not hear any ads, but so far the ads aren't excessive.

This is a great opportunity for ad placement and positioning. Hardly anyone is utilizing this platform right now, and that could be a good thing. Can you come up with a catchy phrase or slogan? Try a Pandora ad and see what happens. Usually a user needs to listen to an ad a few times before they convert into a customer or a client, so don't sell yourself or your company short by not recycling your ad within the same listening cycle.

Click here for more information: http://advertising.pandora.com.

You really can't know what's going to work and what won't, so give Pandora a try.

LinkedIn

LinkedIn is considered the sleeping giant of all the social networks. Not flashy, LinkedIn appeals to white- and blue-collar workers and businesses on the simple premise that it's the largest professional network on the Internet. With 230 million members, they're probably right.

Right now there are more males on LinkedIn than females, and more users than not are college educated and generally have higher incomes.

Similar to other social networks, LinkedIn expects you to fill out a personal profile. Unlike the other social networks, the expectation on LinkedIn is to have a thorough and well-thought-out social profile. The higher your profile strength, the more likely you'll appear in social searches.

LinkedIn suggests you correctly identify your industry and your zip code. You must list your current position with a detailed description. Your education is an important detail, as are your top skills. You should also upload a very professional picture (e.g., not holding your cat, unless you're a veterinarian).

Many people are primarily using LinkedIn to establish job market credibility and to possibly get recruited for a higher-paying job. That's not to say that you shouldn't create a profile and let everyone know what you're doing. Just because you're a 9-to-5 escape artist doesn't mean you shouldn't have a killer profile. People are curious. They want to see what you're up to, and they usually want to see you succeed.

Start requesting to connect with people you already know and those in your sphere. Once you make those connections, you can reach out to those whom you don't know but share something in common with. If you're a freelancer trying to build a bookkeeping business, you'll want to reach out and connect with anyone who may have an interest in your skill set.

Another way to connect with your target market or with other professionals in the same type of business you're creating is to connect in a group. There are thousands of groups on LinkedIn; you just have to do a little searching. You can share your content, search for jobs, and ask for advice. But also join a group that is totally outside of your industry. You can grow your business by offering a different perspective or just by being different from everyone else.

A group is not a company. Don't mistake the two. A LinkedIn group is similar to a Facebook group in that you're all in the group to build a community around a certain topic of interest. If you can't find a group that meets your needs, start one!

The next step on LinkedIn as a 9-to-5 escape artist is to create a company page for your service or business. You'll want to list what your business does, any awards or press releases you have, and updates that are informative to the LinkedIn audience. Business-related content is going to be the most shared information on this network, but that doesn't mean you can't share other information, like sales and upcoming special events. The goal is to keep your sales funnel full by building awareness.

Be careful about what and how often you post to your business page. LinkedIn is hyper-aware of spammy posts, so make sure you are purposeful in your updates and the content you share.

Connect your Twitter account with LinkedIn. Just above the Public Profile link is the Twitter link. When you connect them, every time you post a status update, a Tweet will go out.

You can generate leads by using the LinkedIn Answer tool. You're setting yourself up as an expert, and you're providing value. Who wouldn't want to give business to someone like that? By providing help, you'll in turn generate more business.

How can you use LinkedIn to convert into money for your business? There are a few things to keep in mind. LinkedIn Direct Ads can help you drive traffic to your company page or directly to your website. Visit www.linkedin.com/ads/ to learn how to set up a LinkedIn Direct Ad.

You can also increase reach and awareness of your service or product by using LinkedIn's publishing platform. When you publish an original long-form post to LinkedIn, it becomes part of your professional profile. It's displayed on the Posts section of your profile and is seen by your followers. When your content is shared, you can gain new connections when members not in your network see your content because of the share. To write your first long-form post, simply go to your LinkedIn homepage and click the small pen and paper logo near the top that says, *Publish a post*.

Remember to install the LinkedIn mobile app. If you start talking to a new prospect and they have the LinkedIn app, both of you can open the app, bump your phones together, and seamlessly exchange contact information without having to worry about typing errors. Most people don't know this can be done, so do it!

If you're feeling really confident with LinkedIn, try paying for one of their premium accounts. It's a great way to build a lead list of qualified business prospects. You'll have access to advanced search tools, you can see who's viewed your profile, and you can receive data regarding your accounts and potential leads.

> $mart Tip: A personal page is different from a dedicated page for your business. Visit www.business.linkedin.com/marketing-solutions/company-pages/get-started.html to create a business LinkedIn page.

Klout

Klout is a not so well-known online tool that analyzes an individual's social imprint and influence within a social media network. In essence, it's a grading system of sorts. It's said that if you have a score of forty or less, you'll really need to work on your social media posts and engagement within your communities because you're not very influential. Sorry, don't take it personally. Social media posting is an art form, a skill that needs to be tweaked and refined again and again until you've gotten it just right. And then one of the algorithms will change, and you'll have to figure it all out again.

Within Klout, you will first connect it to some of your other social networks so it can measure your influence. You can connect Twitter, Facebook, Google+, LinkedIn, and many more. Klout scans through your platforms and counts how many people like, +1, comment, re-tweet, re-share, etc. And then Klout gives you a number from one to a hundred. Klout will give you your ninety-day high number for social influence and your ninety-day low number, and your activity shows up in graph form.

The very top social media influencers hover around 82. These people are pros at posting relevant content all the time and know their audience. They interact with a lot of people, and people really trust them. They most likely have a family of trained monkeys living with them, as every single social media site has content posted to it every hour, with replies made to commenters within the hour. These people have bugged-out eyes, and their skin is pale from never seeing the light of day.

You can raise your score by raising your engagement and the effectiveness of your posts. Klout is especially useful in analyzing if the effort you spend online is worth it. The rules of engagement are simple yet difficult to implement because we fail to be consistent. Build your platform by creating awesome, shareable content. Engage and interact with others. If you can't do this on your own, then hire a freelancer to do it for you. Then you'll see a noticeable difference.

Klout isn't another way to make you feel awful about how (un) popular you are or how disinterested your audience is in you. Although there are one or two people who I've taught how to use Klout, and then I see on Facebook that they've ended up at the local bar. If you were growing a garden and you labored over a plant that wasn't producing any fruit, you'd yank it out and focus on something else. Klout helps you identify which of your plants aren't producing and which ones are. Effective social media marketing is focusing on what works and killing what doesn't.

Use Klout to measure if your social media platform is growing in influence. If not, analyze how you can improve and try something different. Use Klout's Look Back tool and see if things are changing for you. Determine what social media platforms you're most influential on and continue doing what looks like positive return on investment for your brand or business.

Fear not. Unlike in high school, online popularity doesn't take into consideration what you look like or whether or not you graduated magna cum laude. You can change your online popularity status by simply changing your text, graphics, or target demographics. And for entertainment purposes only, check your score against the girl from junior high who thought she was hot stuff and put gum in your long hair just for laughs. There's something insanely satisfying when you see no one cares about what she thinks anymore.

Paper.li

According to their website, Paper.li is a "content curation service" that lets you turn socially shared content into beautiful online newspapers and newsletters." Basically, you identify what kind of content you want to curate on Paper.li and where you want to curate it from. You can set the system up to curate daily or weekly. Once the newspaper is completed, Paper.li sends out email notifications and social posts for you, letting others know that the latest edition of your newspaper has been published.

You can set detailed filters for the content you'd like to curate. For instance, if you'd like to curate articles and events around your city, you'd use the keyword Austin or Austin, Texas. Content curation is used by everyone from a hobbyist to a power professional for marketing and staying on top of trends.

Your newsletter is optimized for SEO for discoverability. You can also embed a WordPress widget allowing you to present new content to your readers on a daily or weekly basis. The best part about Paper.li is that it's free, so there's really no reason you shouldn't play around with it.

From a marketing perspective, Paper.li can be an easy way to get in front of your customers without being intrusive. You're basically providing them with content relative to what your product or service is in an easy to read and visually appealing way. Paper.li makes you look like you're on top of your game. It's also very user friendly, so you can set it and forget it. Add it to your marketing arsenal and see what happens.

For more information, visit: Paper.li (yes, that's the web address—there's no .com after it).

Scoop.It

Just like Paper.li, Scoop.It is an online curation and newsletter site. You can find content, publish it in one click, and share it to most of the social media platforms. You can also embed Scoop.It on your website or blog for easy reading for your web visitors. Scoop.It also works with the Buffer scheduling app, so you can easily integrate it within your social media posts calendar.

Scoop.It offers a basic free plan and a few power business plans for an annual fee. Visit www.scoop.it/tutorial for detailed video tutorials on how to use Scoop.It.

Broadcasting and Podcasting

In May of 2014, Edison Research released a report that Americans spend an average of four hours and five minutes every day listening to some form of audio material, with 52 percent of the time going toward broadcast radio. BlogTalkRadio uses the audio niche to enable business owners or service and product producers to connect with their audience.

With BlogTalkRadio, you can create solo shows, interviews, or a question-and-answer segment. Unlike podcasting, which is pre-recorded, broadcasting can be done live or you can pre-record it. You can embed BlogTalkRadio's player code for your show on your website, blog, or Facebook page. It's a great way to display your expertise and a way for your audience to get to know you on a more personal level.

A podcast usually refers to self-contained audio files distributed through an RSS feed. Podcasts offer greater flexibility over broadcasts in that they offer greater flexibility for portability (podcasting app through iTunes).

BlogTalkRadio allows you to upload, edit, and create an audio show fairly easily. You'll want to make sure you have a quality mic and a pop filter. I'm in love with my Yeti mic, which can be purchased on Amazon for around $100. There are definitely cheaper alternatives, but the Yeti produces amazing sound quality. Tools like Audio Hijak Pro or WireTap Studio (OS X) or Total Recorder for Windows will help you record your voice and add customizable sounds.

I've done both podcasting and broadcasting, and there's value in both. Broadcasting is fun because you're live, but for that same reason, it's not fun. People can make mistakes, cough, and otherwise sound ridiculous. I'm somewhat of a control freak, so hosting a live broadcast sort of makes me feel a little anxious. Podcasting can be edited and is therefore safer, although going the safe route is not as exciting.

With both broadcasting and podcasting, you have to pay for a dedicated host to hold your media. I prefer Libsyn (Libsyn.com).

Currently, BlogTalkRadio charges a monthly fee of around $40. To get started using BlogTalkRadio, visit: www.blogtalkradio.com/btr101.aspx.

> $mart Tip: Check out Spreaker.com and Live365.com for more broadcasting choices.

Yelp

Yelp is for location-based businesses. If you ignored my earlier advice about thinking twice about a brick and mortar building and you've opened one up, you're going to want to create a Yelp account. Created in 2004, Yelp is an app that helps users identify brick and mortar retail- and restaurant-based services within a certain parameter. Users rate the businesses based on their experiences, and the reviews follow your business forever.

According to Yelp, it has a monthly average of 135 million unique visitors. It is the commanding social review site to date. Visit the Yelp for Business Owners page on the site to learn how to claim your business. You'll want to do this sooner than later. Check out your competitors to ensure you create a profile that rocks. You can also see why customers might be leaving negative reviews and make sure you address these issues within your own business to prevent negative reviews being posted about you.

When an unprofessional hair stylist ruined my daughter's hair and refused to fix it, you can bet the second thing I did was post a negative review on Yelp (the first thing I did was post a negative review on Google+). Reviews can make or break a business, so if you're on Yelp, you'd better be running a top-notch business. Many businesses don't know they can respond to reviews. You should respectfully address negative reviews so others can see you're taking measures to correct any problems that created the negative review in the first place.

The key to Yelp is using amazing pictures. There's nothing worse than searching for a restaurant or business within my parameter and then not having enough information to make a choice because the business doesn't have any pictures. What if I was craving a donut and two bakeries came up in my search? One of them has a picture of their building, and the other one has ten pictures of donuts. Which one do you think I'm going to go to? A beautiful and well-done photo gallery is a must. Don't skimp on this part!

Business owners also have access to analytics about their performance on Yelp. You can see how much traffic your Yelp profile is getting and how many times you showed up in search results within the platform. You can also identify user actions, such as whether or not users click to your website or check-in to your location using their mobile device.

You can purchase advertising on Yelp and run a Yelp Deal. Take advantage of these tools to increase visibility and to bring in more customers. Visit https://biz.yelp.com for more information on Yelp for Business Owners.

Flickr

Flickr is a goldmine for great visual content. Flickr is an image and video hosting website and something you'll want to integrate into your marketing strategy. Not because you'll want to advertise here, but because most photographers are on Flikr, and it's a great place to find amazing photos for your blog posts. You can use pictures from Flikr if the owner of the photo gives you permission to do so. There are perfectly honest ways to use pictures without having to pay for them. You just have to know the rules.

The organization Creative Commons (CreativeCommons.org) provides access to several image databases to make searching for shareable photos easy to find. Read about the rules and regulations about attribution and sharing photos. Visit http://search.creative-commons.org to search for photos you can use. Make sure you carefully read the attribution section. If within Flickr you see the icon that says, "some rights reserved," you'll want to make sure you give appropriate attribution.

An alternative to searching directly on the Creative Commons website is to visit: www.flickr.com/creativecommons/. See also http://commons.wikimedia.org/wiki/Main_Page, which is a database of 25 million freely usable media files.

I'm all about trying to do things for free, but sometimes you might be in a time crunch and don't have time to perform a search within Creative Commons for a free usable photograph. In those situations, you can always pay a stock photo site for quick and easy access to thousands of paid images. In my humble opinion, it's worth a few minutes to browse Creative Commons for a free picture. Why buy a cow when you can get the milk for free?

Email Marketing

Don't listen to the people who tell you email marketing is dead. I still get marketing materials sent directly to my email inbox, and so do you. Whether I look at them is a different story, but at least there's a chance I might look at an email if it has an enticing tagline. Dismissing (discrediting) the power of email is dumb and will hurt your business. Email lists are like gold, so mine them. If someone has explicitly given you permission to email them by signing up for your email list, then by all means go ahead and email them.

How do you know when an individual is on social media? And even if they're on a social media platform, how will you know which one they're currently browsing? And, if luck is on your side, and you've just scheduled a post to the social media platform they're on, how do you know they even saw your post? Maybe their Twitter feed was moving so fast they missed your amazing post because they have not set notifications for your username. Or, even more likely, maybe Facebook hid your post because you didn't pay to boost it (yes, they do that).

There are a few great choices for web-based email marketing campaigns. **Constant Contact** (ConstantContact.com) has an inexpensive option, and **MailChimp** (MailChimp.com) allows you to use their service for free if you have fewer than two thousand names on your email list. I love MailChimp. There's just something so gratifying about having a monkey give you a high five on your screen after you've successfully sent an email campaign to your email list. MailChimp is easy to use (maybe that's why they chose a monkey to represent them) and easy to set up. You can have an account within a matter of minutes and easily import all of your email contacts from Gmail or whatever email client you use.

MailChimp offers a lot of templates that will help you easily create a professional email. They also offer analytics, so you can track who is opening your email and if anyone clicks on any links within the body of your email. I love this feature and use MailChimp for everything, including my Christmas e-newsletter. I want to ensure everyone actually gets it, and I'll know because I can view the report showing me my email was viewed on another screen.

I recently hosted a very large masquerade ball. I used Eventbrite to track the tickets, but I used MailChimp to track whether or not someone opened my e-invitation. There's nothing worse than someone becoming offended because they thought they didn't receive an invitation to the biggest party of the year. I noticed a handful of people did not even view the email, so I personally followed up with another email and a phone call.

If you use WordPress to build your website, there's a WordPress MailChimp plugin to embed a MailChimp subscribe form directly onto your website. How great is that? The only way you can guarantee your audience will see your message is if you send an email directly to their inbox. It's not even a guarantee, but at least the odds are ever in your favor, and you'll have a fighting chance they'll at least gaze at it.

Here are a few taglines that might get my attention:
» Last chance to sign up for the webinar that will change your life
» 50% off ends in 12 hours!
» Exclusive invitation for ...
» Free ...

Try using one of those fun online tools I mentioned earlier that scramble words to make a funny post. You'll definitely find some catchy and creative taglines using those (but don't use "Fighting Autism the Samurai Way"; I'm taking that one for my next book).

Email your list once a month, unless you're doing something awesome like having a big sale, hosting a Google+ live hangout, if you're going to be on the news, or any other noteworthy event. Lots of business and top content marketers email once a week or more, but you don't need to do that until you have a lot of content on your website and you feel comfortable writing to your audience more often.

If you're hosting a contest or giveaway, consider using Rafflecopter.com. For $9 a month, it's an inexpensive way to organize well-run and professional-looking contests and giveaways. Consider bundling products or services together for a special or discounted price. Everyone loves getting a deal. Alert your email subscriber list about insider-only information, like upcoming sales. Give away free stuff. Don't let someone leave your website without signing up for your email list. Give them something for free. Whether it's a tip or trick or a short eBook, people want something in exchange for them giving your their email address.

No matter how many emails you plan to send to clients or customers, you're missing a huge piece of the puzzle if you're not using a web-based email marketing service. They're easy to use, easy to set up, and they provide the analytics you need to make sure your marketing is performing at its best. Sign up for a service and get started today.

> $mart Tip: **AWeber** (AWeber.com) and **InfusionSoft** (InfusionSoft.com) are other great providers of email campaign services.

YouTube

YouTube is a video-based site owned by Google, so it's for SEO and integrating with Google+. After creating a business account, you'll want to develop your YouTube channel geared specifically toward your target market. You can categorize your videos and add keywords in your video titles and descriptions. Big and small brands and organizations are tapping into the YouTube marketing niche, and you should too.

Three hundred hours of footage is uploaded to YouTube every minute.[8] That's right, I wrote minute. With its new One Channel choice, your platform can be branded across all screens, you can easily turn people into loyal fans and subscribers, and you can ultimately reach an audience you wouldn't have been able to reach otherwise.

First you must create an account. You probably already have one if you have a Google+ account. Visit https://support.google.com/youtube/topic/3024170?hl=en&ref_topic=3024169 for detailed instructions. You'll need to set up a dedicated YouTube channel for your business, and don't forget to upload your logo so your brand is easily identifiable. You'll then need to contemplate what your long-term plan is for your channel.

Viewers usually decide within the first fifteen seconds if they're going to keep watching or not. Grab their attention and let them know quickly what's in it for them. Offer a clear call to action and make it as simple to follow as possible. Encourage sharing, liking, and commenting on your video. Since YouTube is connected to Google, they have an algorithm for searches, so if your audience is doing the right things with your videos, you're going to get ranked higher in searches. Metadata (the information that defines your video) is factored into searches (the description, the title, the tags you give it).

---

8 Source: www.youtube.com/yt/press/statistics.html

YouTube also provides analytics. You'll see numbers for views, watch time, and traffic source (how your viewers discovered you). As with all analytics, you can tweak your YouTube channel based on the numbers. Try to encourage social sharing, since sharing on other social media platforms is one of the most effective ways for people to discover your content.

Not sure how to make a video? My first suggestion is to search within YouTube: "How to make a YouTube video." Honestly, when I don't know how to do something or would like to learn something new, YouTube is usually the first place I go. I'm a visual learner and want to watch how to do something versus being told how to do something. If you have a smartphone or a video cam on your desktop, you can make a video within a matter of minutes. If you're on a mobile device, you can easily send your video via email or upload it using the USB charger/transfer cable.

Apple offers iMovie, and if you're a Windows user, you'll want to use Windows Live Movie Maker or Windows Movie Maker 2.6. There's really no reason you can't make a fairly decent video once you figure out the basics. Make sure you always choose to make your videos public when you upload them. If you choose private, nobody will be able to see them. Private videos can only be seen by up to fifty people, and unlisted videos won't be listed in any of YouTube's search results.

Embed YouTube videos on your blog or website, because it can be a great tool to set yourself apart from your competitors. Your video can be set to automatically play when people land on the page. Simply click on the icons underneath the video within YouTube, and you can cut and paste the embed code directly to your WordPress website.

Personally, I love visiting websites that have videos on them. It just feels way more personal, and it's easier for me to connect with the business or brand. Even though we don't know each other, I end up feeling like we do because a video gives me a visual connection. Watching a video causes my brain and my heart to connect in a way that doesn't happen when I'm just reading your blog text. I encourage you to integrate videos into your marketing strategy. Video marketing is not being utilized as much as it should be, so there's a lot of room to gain dominance over your competitors.

List.ly

List.ly is another online social curation tool. You can curate content on their site or you can integrate it with yours with their WordPress plugin. List.ly can be beneficial in a marketing strategy when used with the intention of building up your community. It is a collaborative authoring tool and a unique form of media (loosely meaning that you're tapping into users you might not have found anywhere else).

The strategy for using a tool like List.ly is to build large and useful lists that others will want to follow, share, and (here's the important part) contribute to. Yes, others can build to your list. Social list platforms far outperform standard text lists. Those are boring. What's not boring is running across extremely helpful information that may or may not change lives. If you provide a list of something that's going to help me in the way I work, play, and navigate life, then I'm going to support you by becoming a fan and sharer of your content.

List.ly, YouTube, and SlideShare all operate under the premise that your content should be findable and shareable. When people visit these sites, they're open to the possibility of finding new content, so you might as well be the one that they find.

With List.ly, your list doesn't have to be perfect. Just start one (and probably more than one). Have one of your lists ask a question.

What are the best books for 9-to-5 escape artists? Ask for help. This not only helps with engagement, you'll also rank for SEO since lists are automatically tagged for search engine optimization. List.ly also offers metrics, giving you the ability to track views and analyze how people are engaging with your lists.

By this time, you may be slightly overwhelmed with all of your marketing choices. Don't be. Tools like List.ly don't take a lot of time once you've set them up, especially if you have a community that's interacting with and posting to your lists. Create a few great lists, embed them on your website, and check them every so often. If you receive a few new visits every day to your website, your initial time was well spent.

SlideShare

According to the SlideShare "about" page, SlideShare is the largest online community for sharing presentations and other professional content. It was founded in 2006 and acquired by LinkedIn in May 2012. Users can upload and share presentations, PDFs, webinars, and other documents. Users can make their uploads private or public, and SlideShare works with files such as PowerPoint, PDF, KeyNote, and other OpenDocument presentations. The slide decks can be viewed on the site, embedded on other websites, or accessed and streamed through mobile devices.

SlideShare gets over 65 million unique visitors a month and ranks among the top 120 most visited websites in the world. It's important to note that SlideShare receives 500 percent more traffic from business owners than Facebook, Twitter, YouTube, and LinkedIn.

BEST PRACTICES FOR SLIDES INCLUDE:
» One message per slide.
» Make sure viewers get your message in under four seconds.

» Use unique but easy-to-read fonts (not Times New Roman, Calibri, Comic Sans).

» Keep your styling consistent, and use no more than three styles per presentation.

» Use great images that convey what you want your audience to know.

» Use complementary colors in your slides. (If you don't understand color theory, I'm sure you can find a presentation about it on SlideShare.)

TRICKS:

» Use your keyword as a filename (when you upload and save, save as the keyword).

» Use your keyword in the title of your presentation, and use that keyword when you add tags to your document.

» Create documents with lists (Top 25, 10 Best, 18 X You Won't Want to Miss).

» Don't make a long presentation. Stick with 24 to 32 slides.

» Post your presentations to other networks, especially LinkedIn and Google+. (You can add your SlideShare to your LinkedIn profile by clicking the edit button on your profile, clicking the box with a plus sign, and then adding the link to your SlideShare slides.)

Tumblr

Tumblr is a micro-blogging site, meaning its content is smaller than a typical blog, usually in the form of very short sentences, one image, or a link to a video. It was created in 2007, and Yahoo purchased it in 2013 for $1 billion (yes, that's billion). It has blogging functions similar to WordPress, social sharing and liking similar to Facebook, and image managing similar to Pinterest, with the exception of only one blog page versus many boards. Interestingly, 65 percent of users have a college education,[9] and 14 percent of high school students use Tumblr daily.[10] Hopefully not while they're in school.

With 20 billion page views a month and 300 million unique visitors and growing, it's a power player for sure. Some people think Tumblr is the grandfather of Pinterest, in that they both attract users who are highly visual. Lifestyle content such as art, fashion, music, and travel are very popular here. If you want to reach an audience with a creative bent that loves to share content, you might want to consider creating a presence on Tumblr.

Tumblr is the most popular social site for people in the United States under twenty-five, thus something you should keep your eye on.[11] There's a lot of porn on this site, so if you have teens, do not turn a blind eye to this one. It's hard to track and find users unless you know their usernames, and even then, you have to be accepted for users to let you into their circle of trust. A huge benefit of Tumblr is there's no mechanism for bullying or trash talking back and forth.

A strategy for Tumblr marketing would be to focus on a very defined niche and link every post to your main website. Use hashtags so users can find your content, and make sure you're following other Tumblrogs (code name for a Tumblr blog) and posting their content on your page to show community support. It's imperative that you interact with followers by reposting and commenting. Connect your Instagram account to easily double your exposure.

---

9 Source: www.statisticbrain.com/tumblr-company-statistics/

10 Source: http://finance.yahoo.com/news/smartphones-boost-us-teens-connections

11 Source: http://blog.garrytan.com/tenth-grade-tech-trends-my-survey-data-says-s

The brain processes images sixty thousand times faster than text, so it's easy to understand why these image social sites are doing so well. Remember, 78 percent of Tumblr posts are photos or images, so create amazing images!

Tumblr really is hit and miss. Some businesses rave about leveraging Tumblr, and some don't. It's hard to tell unless you give it a try.

Google+

Google+ offers personal pages and business pages. Businesses can become verified so that they pop up when potential clients search for location-based services. For instance, if someone types in "business coach, Austin, Texas," if you've verified your business address, you'll pop up. Along with your location, people can see reviews and a link to your website.

Strategies for Using Google+:

» Host Google+ live hangouts for discoverability and to get new customers. You can easily show off your product, teach according to your platform, or connect with readers if you're an author of a new book. Google+ live hangouts are automatically recorded by Google and posted to YouTube (Google owns YouTube). Consider hosting live Google+ hangouts for special clients.

» You can quickly invite a whole bunch of people to connect with you by searching for the keywords "circle share" within Google+ search box.

» Embed a +1 share button on your website and all of your blog posts.

» When sharing content on Google+, make sure to name (or tag) others in the post by typing a plus sign (+) in front of their names. Also make sure to circle the group you want to view the post in addition to making it public. This way, your target group will receive a notification in their email inbox if they've allowed notifications in their Google+ settings.

» Friends+Me app will share your Google+ posts to other platforms (Facebook, Twitter, Tumblr, LinkedIn) and will allow you to cross post to Google+ pages, Twitter, LinkedIn (profiles, pages, and groups), Facebook (profiles, pages, and groups), and Tumblr.

» Join communities and create your own community. Make it public with an easy name. Don't use this for shameless promotion. Encourage and promote sharing of relevant content, interspersing your content at a 90/10 ratio.

» Google+ +1s are the equivalent of a "Like" on Facebook, only more valuable. Google's crawlers scan the web for these links, and the more you rack up, the higher your SEO ranking will be.

» Make the plus button accessible from as many platforms as possible. Integrate +1 onto your website. Fans that +1 can easily share your content on their own pages, helping your SEO rank even more!

» Learn how to get a custom Google+ URL by visiting this web page: https://support.google.com/plus/answer/2676340?hl=en.

Final Thoughts

To sum up, you should:

- » Write original content on your blog (website).
- » Find a free picture for the blog post using Creative Commons or use a stock photo you paid for.
- » Shrink the link using Bitly.com.
- » Login to Hootsuite.com and schedule to share the link on your social networks, including but not limited to Google+, Twitter, Pinterest, Facebook, Instagram, StumbleUpon, and LinkedIn.
- » Track the clicks using Bitly.
- » Link Google Analytics to your website. Once active, check the analytics once a week.
- » Using MailChimp, send a weekly or monthly email to your email marketing list summarizing all of your content and posts for the week or month.
- » Look at MailChimp's analytics to see how many people opened the email.
- » Adjust as needed.
- » Repeat.

Chapter Thirteen

YOUR WEBSITE

WordPress is arguably the best and easiest blogging and content management system on the planet. Everyone uses it, and it's somewhat easy to learn. WordPress has leveled the playing field for individuals like me whose left side of the brain is not as developed as the right side. Now anyone can learn how to launch an amazing website or blog within a day.

A simple way to launch and host your own WordPress website is to first set up a hosting plan with GoDaddy.com. Then you'll want to purchase a domain name. Call GoDaddy support and have them walk you through installing WordPress onto your server. It will take up all of fifteen minutes. Read this for easy instructions: https://support.godaddy.com/help/article/6695/installing-and -activating-your-premium-wordpress-theme.

You can easily choose one of the pre-loaded WordPress templates and immediately begin tweaking your website. If something isn't quite working, you don't have to pay a web developer a fortune to fix it. Visit WPCurve.com for a pay-per-use problem fix, or sign up for one of their monthly plans. You simply let them know what the problem is, and they'll fix it the same day. Done and done!

Have you ever received a request to take action on someone's website, and once you got there, you were confused? There's nothing worse than a cluttered website. It's so important to design your website with an accessible and visible call-to-action button. I love the clean and universal layout of WordPress.

Websites like WPBeginner.com are great resources for how to start a WordPress website, and they have free videos if you're like me and need to watch how to do something versus reading how to do something. Go here for more information: http://videos.wpbeginner.com.

> $mart Tip: If you don't want a WordPress website, check out Wix (Wix.com). Wix offers free website templates, and they offer website hosting packages. Squarespace, Weebly, and Yola also offer website templates and hosting.

Ads

Tread lightly when considering how and when to monetize your website or blog. If you have too many ads, your site will look cluttered. Done correctly, you should have just enough ads to make money but not too many to scare people away.

Visit https://www.google.com/adsense to learn how Google AdSense works and how to implement it on your website. An alternative to AdSense is Chitika (https://chitika.com/about). They only show ads to users when and where they want to see them.

Search Engine Optimization (SEO)

The biggest concern you should have when creating a new business and corresponding website is making certain people will and can find you. Search engine optimization knowledge has become a highly sought-after skill set. SEO specialists can be very pricey to hire but well worth it.

There are also websites like SearchEngineWatch.com that will help you stay on top of search engine optimization techniques and tips. You might really want to consider outsourcing this task to SEO consultants who specialize in ranking your site. Even though it'll be a big expense, their expertise will outweigh how much time, energy, and effort you might be spending in order to learn basic SEO.

Here are a few easy ways to integrate SEO on your website:
» Include a keyword or phrase in your blog post title. Repeat it in the first sentence of your post.
» Whenever you can, reference past blog posts in your new blog posts with a hyperlink.
» Encourage reviews on Google.
» Make sure to register with Google Webmaster tools to make sure your site is SEO friendly (https://www.google.com/webmasters/).
» Remember, your website is your biggest billboard. It is the primary landing spot when people search for you, and it could make or break your business. Don't skip this important step when launching your business. Pay attention to details and hire out tasks if necessary.

$mart Tip: If you use WordPress, install the Yoast or Sociable plugin for SEO. Web hosting service providers such as Weebly offer built-in SEO within their packages.

Landing Page

Squeezing works on more than just lemons. Web landing pages (also called squeeze pages) are pages specifically designed to convert visitors into paying customers. When someone lands on these pages, they either immediately receive a pop-up window that asks them to do something, or the pop-up is activated within a certain amount of time. Usually, the pop-up asks for an email address in exchange for something, like a PDF of tips or a small eBook.

As mentioned before, you don't need to recreate the wheel. Landing pages have proven to be effective, so you should use them, regardless of your opinion about them. I get annoyed with them too sometimes, but that doesn't mean I won't sign up for something because the offer is compelling enough for me to do so.

You don't have to be skilled in the art of web development in order to build a great landing page. A service called LeadPages (LeadPages.net) is one of the best providers around for inexpensive and highly creative squeeze pages. I think it's brilliant that LeadPages understands how people navigate sites, and they've developed a proven system to make sure you have the highest possibility of customer conversion. And no, they didn't pay me to say that. At least read about landing pages and consider the low-cost to high-return ratio. I think you'll easily be won over.

LeadPages can work with both WordPress and HTML files if you don't use WordPress. It integrates with the power players in email marketing (MailChimp and others), and LeadPages provides analytics so you can measure your results.

Most users who actively use LeadPages see their email lists grow by 50 percent within the first few months, and some see growth up to 310 percent over a one-year period. Don't put the cart before the horse though. Make sure you have content on your website and something of value you can offer your clients or customers for opting in. LeadPages has tons of customizable templates, so you don't have to worry about looking like everyone else. All of the professional bloggers use some sort of landing page capture system. It works, so give it a try!

> *When you have exhausted all possibilities, remember this: you haven't.*
> —THOMAS EDISON

Affiliate Marketing with Amazon

Amazon wants to use your website to find new customers. And they'll pay you for it.

What is affiliate marketing and why should you care? It's basically revenue sharing between an online merchant and an online publisher (you). You're compensated based on the result of the click. If someone buys something, you get a percentage of it.

Amazon claims dominance of affiliate marketing because they've been around since 1996. By creating links and options for customer click throughs, you earn a referral fee when someone buys something, starting at 4 percent and up to 10 percent for certain purchases.

Maybe you think you just want a clean website. Nothing but the good stuff (all of your awesome content and products). Would you change your mind if you knew ads and affiliate marketing can earn money for you 24/7 without you having to lift a finger? If done correctly, affiliate ads don't have to be intrusive or annoying. Most readers of blogs nowadays are used to seeing ads on a blog. It's pretty standard. You're not going to offend someone if you have a nice clean widget on the side of your website that says Amazon on it.

The great thing is, you can customize what's shown on your website from Amazon. If you're an author, you can make a subtle slideshow of your favorite books that links directly to them. If you have a travel website, you can showcase items people might want to purchase that are related to travel. If you're a food blogger, you could showcase colorful mixing bowls and kitchen gadgets. If you're a tech consultant, you could display the latest and greatest electronic devices. The key to this is knowing what your audience likes and then turning a visitor to your site into someone who ends up buying something from Amazon. And you get money for it.

Of course, Amazon provides tracking reports on a daily basis. You can learn what other types of products your audience buys and what types of links will motivate them to buy. Amazon is intuitive, with the ultimate end goal of converting someone into a paying customer.

You're not going to get rich quickly using affiliate marketing, but you will notice your sales increase as your web traffic increases. If you're just starting a blog, it might be a little while before you notice nice profits. If you already have an audience that knows and trusts you, you should try to implement affiliate marketing as soon as possible. Otherwise, you're really missing out on an opportunity for a set-it-and-forget-it income stream.

Here's a link for how to set up affiliate marketing: https://affil-iate-program.amazon.com/gp/associates/join/getstarted_second. And here's a link to the official Amazon Associates blog so you can stay on top of the curve: amazonassociates.typepad.com.

Chapter Fourteen

INSURANCE

You wouldn't send your teen off in your car with all of her friends waving in the backseat without having full coverage, would you? Apply this same thought process toward insuring your business. You birthed it, and you've poured blood, sweat, and a few tears into it. Make sure you're insured so you don't lose it. And if you die, you're going to make sure your business partners or your spouse have enough money to keep it going in your absence.

Here are a few options you should consider:
- » **Key-man** (Are you in a partnership or do you have an important person on your team? You should insure them).
- » **Liability** (Everyone is sue happy! You need this).
- » **Error and Omissions** (Because you'll probably make a mistake or two, and as stated above, everyone is sue happy).
- » **Cancer** (No brainer. Everyone is getting cancer. Aflac is awesome, as are others.)
- » **Disability** (Do you really want to take a chance?)
- » **Life** (Term policies expire after a certain amount of time and are usually cheaper than whole life policies that

remain in force over a whole lifetime. Term and whole mixed together is cheaper than whole. Just make sure you have something.)

» **Workman's Comp** (If you have employees, most states require you have this coverage to ensure they have protections if they are injured on the job).

It's a good practice to review your insurance coverages every year. It's a pain in the butt, but you might save some serious cash if you ask your insurance broker to shop around for you. Those few dollars add up over the year. Who knows? You might save enough to buy yourself a few glasses of wine—but not more than three glasses a week, because then you'll get cancer. But you'll have insurance for that, right?

> $mart Tip: Call your local Department of Labor to determine what types of insurance are required by your state when and if you have employees. Some states require workman's compensation insurance to cover independent contractors too.

Chapter Fifteen

A WORD ABOUT HIRING

Fool Me Twice, Shame on Me

Sometimes no matter how many strengths tests, background checks, and referrals you obtain for a specific employee you've hired, you still might end up with someone who becomes a detriment to your business. The key to making sure an unethical employee doesn't derail your business is to not give away the master keys. Make sure your small business continuity log is so detailed and kept up to date that if a key employee leaves, you won't be up a creek. A continuity log is simply a binder or an easily accessible digital file outlining all of the steps and processes necessary to run your business.

Make sure a checks and balances system is implemented with your employees. One person shouldn't have sole access to all bank accounts and passwords, and a system of financial cross-checking at least monthly is a necessary safety step.

I learned this lesson the hard way. In a business I'd been operating with my ex-spouse, we'd hired a woman from our church to answer phones and do the scheduling and books. In my naïveté, I gave her passwords to bank accounts and other very important online payment systems. In my haste to save time, I rarely checked her work, and I did not closely monitor my accounts.

We had a home office at the back of our home with access to our on-site shop and equipment. In the office, we used a filing system that wasn't locked, where I also kept important papers from my childhood, medical records, and past tax documents. Needless to say, this woman became a romantic partner with my ex and funneled money to different accounts without my knowledge. Client accounts were adjusted in the software system where active invoices would be deleted, and when payment came in, she'd just cash in other accounts or go directly to the client's bank and cash the check to eliminate the paper trail.

One day I returned from a business meeting and everything in the office was gone. The whole filing cabinet with my precious papers was gone. The computer was gone, with no backup disk for me to recover my important information. Obviously, this woman is only half to blame, but I take responsibility in that my ignorance and lack of implementing backups and checks cost me more than I'll ever admit.

There's a fine line between trusting someone and spying on them and breaching privacy laws. There are a few things you can do as an employer to monitor what an employee is doing if he or she works in your home or office. Trust should be earned, not automatically given. I dish out trust the same way I give my kids M&Ms when they do something I ask them to do. If a person proves to be trustworthy, then you can boldly give them a little more of you and your business and see how they do.

In retrospect, I should have checked her daily Internet activity log, set alerts on my bank account every time a login was noted, and reviewed invoices printed to cross-check against voided invoices. I should've never given someone my passwords. My important tax documents and cherished papers would have been inaccessible to anyone other than me had they been in a safety deposit box.

Even if you don't have someone working for you right under your nose, there are plenty of ways to guard your property, proprietary rights, and the business you've worked so hard to build. In our state, we have no-compete clauses between an employer and an employee. They really don't hold up all that much, but you can still scare the pants off someone and make them sign one when you hire them (if it's legal to do so in your state). Going to court costs thousands of dollars if this contract is breached, but simply having an attorney draft a letter stating the other person is in breach of contract might be a low-cost way to get them to stop.

I'm still a trusting person. I always give others the benefit of the doubt—with parameters. A person can make the same mistake twice, but when a business owner makes the same mistake twice, it's not a mistake; it's a choice. If I know the repercussions of not protecting myself and my business, and I don't take steps to prevent it from happening, it's my own damn fault if something bad happens. I don't give independent contractors or anyone who's doing anything for me on the business level any opportunities to harm me or my business.

Someone once told me that, sometimes, giving someone a second chance is like giving them an extra bullet for their gun, since they missed you the first time. I'm all about forgiveness and not holding on to bitterness and all of that. Bitterness just clogs up your creativity and optimism. There are a lot of companies that have a second- and third-chance policy for their employees. I don't. You can forgive someone in your heart, but you don't have to forget what they've done. If someone lies or steals from you, then in my humble opinion, you need to give them the boot. They can go and work on improving their ethics on their own time. You're trying to build a 9-to-5 escape artist lifestyle, and you don't want someone else's garbage stinking up your life.

Just in case you're wondering, the secretary and the ex only lasted a few short months, and the business died fairly quickly. I was mostly sorry for the clients and spent many hours on the phone doing damage control while concurrently going through a divorce. I didn't care I lost the business. I got my kids, kept all of our friends, and got out of there. I have an amazing life now. I'm living proof you can lose everything, but you can overcome, rebuild, and enjoy a ridiculously abundant life.

We all go through things for a reason, and I'm wiser from my past experiences. Now it's easy for me to spot questionable behavior, and I've been able to help other businesses set up fail-safes for protection from ethically challenged employees. So ultimately, what happened to me has helped hundreds of other people in the long run. It's lose-win-win.

> *Trust is like an eraser;*
> *it gets smaller and smaller*
> *after every mistake.*
> —UNKNOWN

$mart Tip: Install keystroke software on your office computer. Schedule automatic backups to the cloud. You'll never have to worry about someone walking away with your information.

Smart Practices

You can't expect your independent contractors or your employees to care as much about your business as you do. It's just not going to happen. No matter how much you pay them, I promise none of them will stay up at night as long as you will worrying about the business. They won't cry a river if you lose a major contract (unless it affects their pay), and they won't be there to help bail you out if you get audited.

Whether we admit it or not, no one is as important as we are to ourselves. Of course we would die for our children, and we'd donate a kidney to our spouse if totally necessary, but ultimately we really care about ourselves first and foremost. God put survival instincts into us for a reason. We are all highly skilled in the art of preservation tactics.

Your employees and independent contractors won't be with you forever. Yes, they will job jump if they receive a much better offer from someone else. Sure, loyalty goes really far, but at the end of the day if someone can upgrade from hamburger to filet mignon, then they will do it. Every time. It's a no brainer. Taking all of this into consideration, the following are some smart practices to implement:

» Don't share too many secrets. It's okay to make a continuity log for your employees, but don't give them access to yours. Your continuity log should be private with the exception of your business partner(s). Don't give an employee access to your bank statements or tax records, and don't give them login credentials for financial accounts.

» Invest in your employees so they won't want to leave or take your ideas and build their own copycat model. Reward their hard work with bonuses, trips, random gifts of thanks, etc.

» Give ownership to your employees so they are further vested in the success of your business. Sell them shares in your company after a certain period of time. (Check with your accountant or an attorney how to do this correctly.)

» Hold employees accountable.

» Don't leave opportunities open for employees to take advantage.

» Set up parameters and checks and balances (for example, make them turn in receipts and follow protocol every time).

» There's absolutely nothing wrong with asking potential future job applicants to take a strengths (or personality) test. This is your business, and finding the right people to do work for you is integral to your success.

Wonder Woman has a Virtual Assistant

A virtual assistant (VA) is someone who does work for you without having to be in the same location as you. They are not location based; they simply have to have access to the Internet. English may or may not be their primary language. Virtual assistants can and will do great work for you if you screen them appropriately. They can work on projects anywhere at anytime. They simply take orders or directions and accomplish tasks for you. Virtual assistants are like mini-me's of you, because you've trained them how to get work done for you with close to the same result you'd produce. You are producing concurrently, so you're getting twice as much done. Two brains are better than one, twenty fingers are better than ten ... you get the idea. In the same way women wish they could have their own housewives, a virtual assistant gets all of your crap done so you can do something else.

I've touted VAs for years, yet the concept is only recently taking off. It's hard to pay someone money when you think you can do simple tasks yourself. In my humble opinion, by not hiring a VA, you are stepping over dollars to pick up pennies. It just makes more sense to hire someone for less money than you make per hour to have them accomplish tasks that can be delegated.

You must first determine what your highest and lowest value tasks are. List them in numerical order. When you get to task seven or eight, analyze whether or not you could delegate the task to someone else. For instance, it would be important for me to personally return a phone call from someone who has been referred to me by a current client. If I'm going to be speaking to their employees about productivity or social media marketing strategies, the client is going to want to initially speak directly to me to see if I'm a good fit for them or not. I'm not going to have a VA talk for me. Alternatively, if I get my voicemails transcribed by GoogleVoice or another similar provider, I can forward voicemails from current clients who have a quick question to my VA to make sure they receive personal service. I can also have my VA answer simple web inquiries, assist my social media marketing clients with instructions as to how to access their social media sites or how to appropriately interact with their audience online, etc.

VAs can be helpful in any capacity. Even if you have employees, you still might want to have a VA to ensure your personal life is well organized. I sometimes believe some of my stay-at-home-mom friends who don't run a business need to have a VA to organize their schedules and make appointments for them. It's hard running a household, and you need all the help you can get! Sometimes you can find a VA for less than minimum wage. I wouldn't expect a whole lot for that price, but it's better than not having one at all. Good ones can be found for an average of $9 an hour and up, depending on their skill set.

I have a few great ones in my back pocket who just love taking work whenever I have some to give. They don't get angry if I don't consistently have work for them because they're working for a lot of other people too. One of my favorites is a beautiful girl I met at a writing critique group. She'd just graduated from college with a BA in literature. She was heading to a different state to roam the Pacific Northwest and was interested in learning how to post for others on social media. I taught her the ins and outs remotely. I didn't spend much time using screenshots and video conferencing, yet she learned very quickly. Now she's a pro and loves having the flexibility of working from her laptop. It's a win-win for both of us.

It just makes sense to hire out things that take up your time when your time is better spent procuring more business or doing tasks that bring in the most money. It's really hard to implement this concept because we always think we can handle everything our-selves. It's a big, fat lie. We can't do everything ourselves. Doing so will steal your time and your joy. If you're questioning the feasibility of having someone else do online tasks for you, just try it for a few weeks and see if your life changes or not. Since VAs are independent contractors, you can let them know in advance it might only be a few weeks' worth of work, and that's it. I can tell you right now you're not going to be sorry you hired a VA (unless you get a crappy one, then you might). Screen your VAs to determine their experience, creative and critical thinking skills, and customer service skills. Ask them to provide work samples and references. Be definitive and not vague when you give them tasks. Set time limits for tasks and have them check in with you often until they prove they don't need to.

Because I don't have a brick and mortar office, people don't see the inner workings of my businesses. It's hard to understand how tasks are delegated and how so many things can be done by one person (they can't). When someone asks me how I can accomplish so much, I initially tell them because I'm a superhero. Since child-hood, I've secretly wanted to be Wonder Woman. Lynda Carter's red boots and skimpy outfit were hot. If you don't know what I'm talking about, stop right now and go look her up. Anyway, after reluctantly admitting that I'm not really a superhero in disguise, I let them know I have virtual assistants to help ensure everything runs smoothly. Then it all makes perfect sense. Admitting how I get life done removes my pedestal, but I have to give credit to my amazing team of VAs. Behind a strong and happy businesswoman is a bunch of VAs and maybe a housecleaner or two.

Want to try hiring a VA? Here are a few places to start:
» EAHelp.com
» Elance.com
» Fivrr.com
» HireMyMom.com
» Ivaa.org (International Virtual Assistants Association)
» Odesk.com
» WritersAccess.com (writing services)
» In its quest for world domination, Amazon also offers an on-demand, scalable workforce to anyone in need: https://www.mturk.com/mturk/welcome.

$mart Tip: Check out these websites for more online customer-care solutions:
» www.westinteractive.com — call routing and customer care
» www.liveops.com/product/liveops-chat — online customer chat solutions
» www.liveops.com/product/liveops-voice-call-center — call routing solutions

Chapter Sixteen

COMPANY MANAGEMENT

Continuity Log

I have to give my husband credit for turning me on … to continuity logs. The log is different from a continuity plan, primarily used to ensure a business will go on in case of a catastrophic or unplanned event. Managing two children is a piece of cake compared to managing three or four children. Something just changes after that second one, and life turns chaotic. His amazing left brain suggested we create a continuity log that we would constantly tweak as we went along. It would include all of our important procedures and operating standards, so to speak. It would also be extremely useful if one of us died unexpectedly; the other person would know exactly how to keep the family running. So, we have a huge three-ring binder with colored, labeled tabs for ease of use. We also store a copy of the continuity log in case someone steals the binder.

Here are a few examples of tabs you might want to create within your business continuity log:

 » Social media accounts and postings protocols

» Interoffice communication protocol
» Customers or client interaction protocol (emails, phone, texts)
» Approved graphics for use in advertising
» The business marketing plan
» What a normal business day looks like
» What tasks are done on a daily, weekly, monthly, quarterly, and yearly basis
» How records are stored and how to access them
» Purchases necessary to keep the business running
» Monthly subscriptions and services
» Press release templates
» Email templates (offers, announcements, giveaways)
» The companies you use for all business systems and operations (listed alphabetically, with account numbers, websites, and phone numbers listed next to each one)
» Banks you use (but put passwords in a different location; you only want to give enough information where someone can pick up where you left off but can't embezzle)
» Protocol for interacting with the media

If you're injured or otherwise unable to run your business, it'll be so much easier for someone else to come in and help out if you have a continuity log available. No matter if your business is a business of one (you) or of many, a continuity log will ensure your business is safe and can go on with little interruption should something catastrophic happen.

Also, consider giving someone you really, really trust financial power of attorney so they can take care of your finances if you are out of commission (if you don't have a spouse or if your spouse is out of commission the same time that you are).

Basecamp

My life forever changed once I was introduced to Basecamp. Really. Basecamp is a web-based project management application that can integrate projects with the people who work on the projects and also people who request the project (clients). The platform is super easy to use and makes task accomplishment so doable. Basecamp works with all platforms and integrates with email. They also offer an app so you can manage everything effortlessly with your mobile device.

You simply log in, create a new project, and invite others to the project. You can have easy-to-follow discussions with everyone on the project, post project updates, and post to-do lists. The to-do lists can be assigned to certain people on the project, and once they're accomplished, the person can mark them done. Files can be uploaded and stored within the project, as well as text documents you create within the project. My favorite feature is you can forward emails from your email client right into Basecamp, saving a lot of cutting and pasting.

Basecamp will revolutionize the way you work and accomplish projects. Clients who use Basecamp with you will be blown away by the efficiency of it. No longer do you have to constantly field questions about the status of a project. The client can easily see what's going on within a project, and you have the ability to hide some of the discussions you're having with other team members from the client if you want to.

I seriously wish my kids knew how to use Basecamp. I can only imagine how organized a family would be if when they all woke up in the morning they logged in and viewed their tasks and to-do lists, checking them off as they went. No one would forget an important task or event. Ever. A mom can dream.

Seriously, you need to check out Basecamp. They offer different pricing models based on how many active projects you typically have going on. If you are a solopreneur or consultant, the ten active projects account for $20 a month at the time of this printing might work for you. Honestly, I'd recommend Basecamp to anyone regardless of whether they owned a business or not. I use it for business and personal projects. I probably just saved you from weeks of disorganization. Pay it forward and go tell someone else about Basecamp, and you'll make a new forever friend. You're welcome.

Chapter Seventeen

PRODUCTIVITY

Have you ever gone to bed and visually walked through exactly what the following day is going to look like? Maybe you've created a list of the tasks you must accomplish, possibly breaking them down into subcategories or labeling them with numbers from one to ten. You set your alarm for five a.m. with the expectation that tomorrow will be your most productive day yet. And then something crazy happens, like your kid wakes up throwing up every hour, and you're still awake when your alarm goes off in the morning. Even though the sun is up, the new day isn't looking as bright as it was the night before.

Despite our best intentions, we hardly ever seem to accomplish everything on our task list. What's a 9-to-5 escape artist to do? You just have to suck it up and figure out one or two of the top tasks and get them done *no matter what*. As mentioned earlier, I also strongly suggest employing a virtual assistant. It's well worth paying someone $9-$18 an hour (depending on experience) if it means important tasks get completed on time and you stay on top of your game.

One strategy highly effective people use is time blocking. Using this strategy, you block out a certain number of hours every morning, and you don't do anything else until that task is accomplished. The effectiveness of this concept is tied to your dedication to completing the task at all costs. You absolutely can't digress. If you are slightly ADD like me, you'll need to implement fail-safe measures like installing an app like Anti-Social (Anti-social.cc) that blocks you from the Internet for certain amounts of time.

As an example, I had to wake up two hours earlier than normal to get this book finished. With four kids, three animals, and one husband to attend to, it would've taken ten years to finish this sucker, and by then it'd be outdated anyway. I had to turn off the Internet, hide my phone, and focus on pounding on the keys for two hours straight. If one of the kids woke up too early, I'd plop them into bed with my husband, for him to deal with. If the dog needed to go pee, I'd just push the shut-up button on my remote-control dog shocker.

On the extremely rare occasion that one of my teens would come downstairs before 7 a.m., I'd simply say, "Power hour," and they knew by then that to speak to me during that time would bring upon them a wrath like no other. And no mall money for a week, which is just as bad.

I know a few people who absolutely can't get a single thing done. You check in with them, and they'll let you know they're working on something or would like to work on something. Then, two weeks later when you talk to them again, they're in the same place. Nothing got done. What happened? I call it fear by analysis. They were thinking about all of the things related to getting that thing done, so they didn't do any of them.

Another popular method for accomplishing tasks is the Pomodoro technique. You need to have access to a timer to do this correctly. First, you choose a task to accomplish. Then you set the Pomodoro (the timer) to twenty-five minutes. You work on the task until the Pomodoro rings, and then you put a checkmark on a piece of paper. You will then give yourself a short break (five minutes) and start another process, taking longer breaks if necessary. If you are distracted during a Pomodoro, you have to start again (good luck if you have little kids!).

Just as I inform my family not to speak or look at me during a power hour, it's important that you communicate to those around you that you can't be distracted during your Pomodoros. Here are a few apps to help you in your quest for Pomodoro dominance:

» Tomighty www.tomighty.org
» Eggscellent www.eggscellentapp.com
» Focus Timer (available in the iTunes app store)

When I hear people lamenting about not getting anything done, I secretly think, *Get over yourself and quit making excuses.* (Not a secret anymore, I suppose.)

Author and motivational speaker Jim Rohn says, "If you really want to do something, you'll find a way." I put this saying on a Facebook banner I use for my personal page. I do this because I want to remind everyone who comes in contact with me that I won't accept excuses. Unless you have a serious debilitating disease, you can and will find a way to do the things that need to get done. If you don't, you don't really care enough about the request or the task at hand.

I have a special-needs kid, and I can still manage to find the time to finish tasks. If I can clean my house (sometimes), remember to send out birthday cards, sit on boards, and run businesses, then you can do some of those things too. There are people with way more disadvantages than dealing with special needs who find the time to do great and not so great things. The ones who get crap done put their hearts, minds, bodies, and souls into their efforts and have an all-in mentality.

Some people can self-regulate, and others need to teach themselves how to be effective time managers. If you are an individual who needs to be observed to stay on task (i.e., the Hawthorne effect, which states some work better when others are observing them), then by all means ask someone to point-blank ask you every day what you accomplished. To finish this book on time, I had an accountability partner ask me every Monday at 9:15 a.m. how many words I'd written. Peer pressure works!

The point of all of this is that you have to figure out what you need in order to be the most effective with your time and productivity. Keep trying different techniques until something works for you. If you need help being productive, own it. Hire a coach or ask someone to hold you accountable.

There's a difference between being busy and being productive. Busy people just run around and act like they're being productive, but at the end of the day, they have nothing to show for their busyness. Productive people learn how to accomplish tasks in the least amount of time with the highest efficacy rate possible. Can you see the difference? Be productive, and it will pay off in the form of your business's balance sheet and result in more focused time when you are with those whom you care about the most. Now, who doesn't want that?

Strategies to Use with Clients

I'll let you in on a little secret. I never answer my phone when someone calls me. Ever. Unless it's my husband or one of my children. I always let the calls go to voicemail and then listen to the message or wait for Google to send me an email with their voice message. Answering phone calls you're not expecting is a huge time-suck. If you don't let the calls go straight to voicemail, you're mismanaging your time.

Once you listen to the voicemail, hopefully you can quickly identify what the person wants. Then you can instantly determine how best to deal with the caller and the reason for the call. Most of the time, I'll do one of two things: If the person calling is already a client, I'll text or email the person and thank them for their phone call and answer their question via text or email, letting them know I'm unavailable to talk. This way the person's need is met and they don't feel neglected. If the person is a new client, I'll text them and thank them for their phone call, let them know I'm in a meeting, and ask them what the best time to call them back is. This way they know I'm on top of my game, and I haven't lost them before we even get to talk.

Another strategy I use with current clients is letting them know at the beginning of the conversation how many minutes I have to talk. If I only have fifteen minutes, I'll tell them ten because inevitably they'll push for more talk time. At the ten-minute mark, kindly cut them off after a pause in conversation and say: "It's been so nice talking with you today. I've got to let you go now to make my next consultation, but I'll follow up with you in an email by tomorrow."

This way you're setting parameters for your time and you're validating them with a follow-up email. If you do this *every time* you speak with someone, you'll naturally train them to expect your wrap-up of the conversation, and they will know they can always discuss more within an email. Feel free to use this tactic on long-winded friends and family if you're like me and don't enjoy one-hour conversations about what people had for lunch that day.

Remember, you're building a business that will ultimately give you freedom to determine what you do with your time. You have to guard your time as if you're protecting the crown jewels. Don't let anyone steal time from you without your permission.

> $mart Tip: GoogleVoice has a way you can get your voice-mails transcribed into an email. This is super helpful when you're in meetings or in a situation where you're unable to pick up your phone. It also works great when you don't want to speak with those who make you feel uncomfort-able or who are rude to you (ex-spouses come to mind here).

Backup Systems

There's nothing worse than having an amazing session of produc-tivity and losing all of the work you did over the last two hours when your toddler steps on the button on your power strip cord to your computer and wipes everything away. There are so many easy ways to ensure that doesn't happen (the data loss, not the toddler stepping on your stuff).

Here are some options:
- » Use Dropbox (Dropbox.com) for cloud storage and data backup.
- » Carbonite.com can help with backing up your entire com-puter and offers seamless recovery.
- » Other cloud backup sites include: SpiderOak.com, IDrive.com, and MiMedia.com (for media files).
- » If you're an Apple user, use the time machine feature and schedule regular backups to an external USB drive.
- » Use Google Drive backups and schedule them to regularly sync with your desktop and laptop.

» Set backups to your backups. You can never be too careful. This also comes in handy when you're traveling because you can easily access all of your files from the cloud no matter what your location. Make it easier on yourself. Take ten minutes right now and back up your stuff.

Joel Lund, CEO Prepare For Rain, LLC
9-to-5 escape artist

Growing up, Joel dreamed of being a writer. He loved to read about magical places and creatures. Or about artists, because he loved to draw, and people told him he was good at it. The very last thing he expected was to become a pastor, and even less so … a businessman.

Of course, that's what happened. After earning a master's degree, he wanted to teach at a university while completing a PhD. Hundreds of applicants fought for those positions. Many rejections later, Joel decided he could influence young people as a youth pastor. Even with his background and education, his salary was low. When Joel's wife, Janet, became pregnant with the child they were told they'd never have, he knew a major job change was critical.

Because by then, Janet was the youth minister, and Joel worked part-time in a bike shop so he'd be available to help her out. Consequently, Joel and Janet were a financial train wreck just as they were becoming parents. His aspiration of being a writer hadn't diminished over the years. Yet this dream had been delayed by decades of waiting, wishing, and withering. Dreams don't live in barrenness. But he didn't know how to pursue them. As fulfilling as working with kids was to Joel, there was still a cost. And now a child was coming.

Focused like a hound on the hunt, Joel chose financial services. He knew several people working in the industry, and they didn't seem any smarter than he was. But they clearly made more money than he did. A lot more. Out of desperation, he applied to a national financial planning firm. He was hired. This began a career spanning fourteen years. As a District Manager, his small rural office placed in the top five (out of 400). Later, as a Managing Principal, his division averaged $30M per year, managed $500M in assets, and served thousands. Joel received international recognition within the industry and multiple awards from his firm.

However, the work nearly killed him. Literally. The stress was enormous, the demands relentless. Gratitude was nearly non-existent. His "successful" career was a J. O. B. He'd been successful because he had to be.

With Janet's encouragement, he walked away. It was true that after fourteen years in his business career, their financial reality had improved. The contrast with their years in ministry, which left them a hot mess financially, was extreme.

Still … he knew there had to be a better way, a pathway where passion and purpose could merge together.

In under three years, Joel formed two companies, published three books, and earned two coaching certifications. He has conducted numerous workshops and training courses for entrepreneurs of all kinds, with a special emphasis toward those seeking to reach beyond their J. O. B. and diligently expand their creative impact.

Every day, he and Janet lean hard into all things entre-preneurial. It's a lot of work. Perhaps even more work than at the height of his career stress. But the reward is tre-mendous. No longer does a J. O. B. keep him from almost everything that mattered to Joel: his family, his dreams, his purpose, and his creative pursuits. Now his focus is on making a positive difference in the lives of others, bring-ing hope, transformational tools, and encouragement. Prepare For Rain delivers the just-in-time coaching and resources that gutsy, creative people want to move more fully into their passions, so their stories get into the world. You can download his complementary eBook, *Reclaim Your Dream* at: http://www.prepareforrain.com/reclaim-your-dream/. Let your transformation begin!

Chapter Eighteen

METRICS

Insanity: doing the same thing over and over and expecting different results.
—ALBERT EINSTEIN

Bitly

How do you know for sure what's working within your social media posts and what's not? Do you keep doing the same thing, expecting different results? There is a solution to help you determine if what you're doing is working, and the solution has a name: Bitly (Bitly.com).

Bitly is currently the largest URL shortening service on the web. It takes very long web URLs and shortens them to a manageable size, making the link easy to share and easy to remember. The link is also trackable, providing insights into clicks and where the clicks are coming from. Anyone who clicks on the link will be redirected to the original URL and its content.

When you sign up for a free account with Bitly, you can use the insights to check how your link performed compared to other Bitly links directing to the same content. You can access analytics within the Bitly website or simply add a + sign to the end of your link (http://bit.ly/AUgv+). When you visit the statistics for your links, you'll have access to a bar graph to track how your link is doing every day. Older links can even be viewed by the hour.

A few years ago, I decided to try an experiment. I wondered how many people on my Facebook page were really looking at my shared content versus just liking the content or not engaging with it at all. Unless someone physically clicks the like button, you have no idea if you're sharing something people care about or not. For one week, I shortened all of my links before I posted content. If I shared a video from YouTube, I'd shorten the link and track. If I shared a blog post, I'd do the same thing. I was pleasantly surprised to find the majority of my audience was actually clicking on the links. Factoring in the amount of "friends" I had, at least 75 percent of them were clicking on my links.

Bitly has been a strong tool in my social media arsenal. After consistently using it when posting to social media, I have a very solid grasp as to what my audience likes to see from me the most. Very rarely do I ever have a post bomb, because I've identified what works and what doesn't. So be encouraged. Just because your fan page only shows five likes on a post, it doesn't mean that people aren't engaging. You might be surprised to know that 289 people clicked and read what you posted, and they just didn't take the time to acknowledge it with a "Like."

Google Analytics

Google Analytics is a free service offered by Google that provides you with statistics and analytical tools to help maximize search engine optimization (SEO). For marketing purposes, this tool will give you insight into what is working within your marketing strategy and provide you with details about your audience and their needs and wants. You'll know the length of time people are viewing your web pages, where they came from, and what they end up doing once they're on your site. Learn more about why you should use Google Analytics by visiting: google.com/analytics/why/.

Within Google Analytics, there's a way to track which social media platform your leads are coming from. This information is supremely useful because you won't be wasting your time on a social media platform that might not be converting into sales or new clients for you. If you notice many leads are coming from Pinterest and very few leads are coming from Twitter, you can adjust your social media marketing strategy based on this knowledge. For in-depth instructions about how to integrate Google Analytics with your social media marketing campaign(s), visit SocialMediaExaminer.com/google-analytics-custom-campaigns/.

If you don't have the time or the desire to learn about Google Analytics, you can find a Google Analytics specialist at google.com/analytics/partners.

The whole point of using analytics within your business marketing

The most effective growth strategies are integrated with actual data.

strategy is to prevent unnecessary time waste. As a 9-to-5 escape artist, your time is precious to you. It's pointless to spend your time doing things that aren't productive, and if you don't utilize analytics and aren't reviewing the results, you won't know what's working and what's not working. The most effective growth strategies are integrated with actual data. If you take the time to set this up properly and have a system in place to periodically review the metrics, you can adjust where you spend your time and focus on what makes you the most money.

$mart Tips:

> » Install the Google Analytics app on your smart-
> phone so you can easily view real-time analytics
> for all of your websites and blogs.
> » Read the PPC Hero blog for tons of informative
> articles about business analytics. Visit: ppchero.
> com/category/analytics/.
> » SemRush.com is a company that can provide you
> with deep digital research and business intelli-
> gence for a fee.

===

Chapter Nineteen

TRADITIONAL WAYS TO GROW YOUR BIZ

Press Releases

Don't make the mistake of thinking you can type up a spiffy one-page press release and everyone on the planet who cares about press releases will read it. With that said, go ahead and write a press release anyway and upload it to your website. It'll make you appear somewhat put together. Title the page "Media Kit" and give your backstory, a high-resolution picture of you they can download, your social media sites, and whatever else you think people might care about. I personally don't ever read those pages, but someone might read it someday when you're super famous, so you should probably do it now before you get too busy.

Check out this free tool from PR NewsWire that will generate a press release for you based on the data you insert into each text box: toolkit.prnewswire.com/pressreleasewizard/.

Networking Meetings

I feel the need to warn you, which is why I'm bothering to include networking meetings here. A chamber or networking meeting is such an unoriginal marketing tactic that I think it may have started in the caveman days. It will take a long time for you to grow your business if you think handing out your business card to other people who are there to hand out their business cards will generate a sale. Unless you are going to a networking meeting with the likes of Donald Trump, I suggest spending your time doing something much more productive.

Trade Shows and Conferences

I speak at conferences all the time. It's a predictable and steady way to grow your business. The trick is to be interactive and make an impression while you're at one. A *good* impression. Have you ever gone to a trade show and walked by a booth where the person sitting behind the table is staring right past you? Their eyes say they've left the building, but their body is still there. Conferences and trade shows have the capacity to turn people into zombies, but only if you don't have a strategy for working them.

The only rule is don't be boring and dress cute wherever you go. Life is too short to blend in.
—PARIS HILTON

If you're going to be a speaker at a conference or if you have a table at an upcoming trade show, tell people! Get on your social media and hashtag (#) the city and the name of the conference in your posts. Tell the universe how excited you are about the event. You probably have access to the conference schedule and those who have a booth alongside you. Connect with them on social media. Make friends before you get there. Be social and fun. People will like you before they've even met you.

Right when you get there, take a picture of yourself at the airport. Selfies are acceptable when they're done with purposeful intent. Continue to hashtag the name of the conference and the city as you make your way to the conference. Nowadays, conferences have official hashtags for tweeting while at the conference. You work that hashtag like a boss and tag everyone else who uses that hashtag throughout the conference. You can bet your booth will be a lot fuller for it.

When you speak, make sure to let people know you'd like to connect with them at your booth. Tell them you have something special for them (a coffee cup, a pen, a PDF of helpful information, whatever). Connect with the people right next to your booth. Ask them why they're there and let them know what you do. Send people to your neighbors' booths, and they'll reciprocate. When people walk by your booth trying to avoid eye contact because they don't want to stop, go around your booth and greet them with a compelling question.

For instance, if I was trying to get people to buy and read this book, I'd say something like, "I have a great cheat sheet for people who're trying to get away from the 9-to-5 time suck and have more flexibility. Can I give you one?" They're not going to say no. Make sure all of your social media and contact information is on the sheet (and a link to your service or product). If they still want to get away from my booth after I've explained the PDF and they don't seem interested in buying my book, I'd try something else.

Maybe I'd ask them if they'd like to receive an email once in a while of tips and tricks to save more time during the workweek. If you provide enough value to someone, they'll want to receive what you're offering. Emails are like gold. If you can successfully obtain someone's email address with their permission, you've hit the jackpot. While they're signing up to receive emails from you, talk to them. Ask leading questions. Ask them why they're at the conference, what they're getting out of it, what they hope to get out of it. You can find out a lot about people by just asking the right questions.

If they use money as an excuse to get out of buying your service or product, give them alternatives. "Don't have any cash? Lucky you, I have a PayPal credit card swiper." If I'm a business coach, maybe I'll offer them fifteen minutes for free. If I'm a social media consultant, maybe I'll offer to look at their website to see if their social media widgets are prominent enough to lead to conversion. If you have their website, you'll usually have access to their email, and if not, get it. No doesn't always mean no; sometimes it just means "not right now" or "I need more information to see the value."

Make sure the banner behind you clearly defines what people are supposed to do at your booth. How many times have you walked by a booth at a conference and, after seeing the name of the business with no explanation, thought, *Okay, next*? How am I supposed to know what "Advanced Solutions" means? Solutions for what? I greatly dislike vagueness. If you don't explain what you do within the two seconds I'm walking past your table, you may or may not get a snarky question, like, "So are you like a super awesome developer creating advanced solutions for taking out terrorist groups who are trying to infiltrate the United States? Because I really think that's awesome. No? Hmm, hard to tell from your sign. I like what I thought you did better."

Don't go to a conference or a trade show and be a dud. That's not the highest and best use of your time and money. Have a strategy and make friends. Offer something of value and do whatever it takes to gather email addresses. Play to your strengths and fake it till you make it. Dressing cute doesn't hurt either.

Even though trade shows are par for the course in standard business growth, they don't have to be a total time-suck. You can connect with a lot of great people, and your business will be all the better for it. Be focused and intentional, and you'll be happy with the results.

Cold Calling

Just don't do it. Ever.

The odds are not ever in your favor that calling random strangers will result in a high sales conversion ratio. Don't listen to anyone who tells you cold calling is effective. Focus on inbound marketing instead. Invest in search engine optimization for your blog or website and pay for Google ads to direct people searching on the web toward you.

Business Cards and Promotional Materials

Handing out your business card is a traditional way to grow your business. It's just a professional courtesy to give someone your contact information on a well-done business card. Until everyone gets on the digital bandwagon, business card printers will remain in business.

Make your business card so unique that people will want to frame it and look at it every day. Make an offer on the back of the card that if they go to your website and sign up for your email list, they can get exclusive offers, discounts, and free stuff. Offer a drawing via Rafflecopter.com once a month, and you can give someone something like one free coaching session or a small eBook listing helpful time-management strategies and apps. Tell them about the offer when you hand them your card and make it so compelling they'll do it right away. If you can, try to list your social media usernames on your cards so potential customers can easily find and connect with you. You should attempt to have as much information as possible on your business card without the text looking bunched together.

Done correctly, a business card should end up causing a person to reach out to you, either through email or through your website. Make sure when you hand someone your business card, you get theirs in exchange. The CamCard app will allow you to easily scan a business card with your smartphone and store contact information. At the end of the day, always send the person an email telling them how nice it was to meet them, and give them your contact information should they ever need anything in the future.

When it comes to your business card and other promotional material, be different and do things others aren't doing. It's the only way you'll stand out from the crowd. Don't be boring when it comes to your paper products. Your branding and identity designs should be creative and immediately catch potential customers' attention. Your visual identity can be an asset for your business, setting you apart from your competitors. Hire a graphic designer to come up with a great logo or pay someone on Fiverr.com to do it. There are so many creative people on Fiverr who just want some business, so you can easily find someone to spiff up your stuff.

If you want some really great ideas for business cards, check out Pinterest. Just type in "business cards" plus whatever business you've decided to go into. You'll get so many amazing ideas your head might explode. You can always use a template, but if you do, please pick a catchy one. Here are a few fun websites with really unique card templates:

- » SeeJaneWork.com
- » Minted.com
- » Etsy.com (type in "business card templates")
- » Zazzle.com (also great for creating branding paraphernalia)

At conferences and trade shows, it's always fun to have cool branding items to pass out. They certainly can be expensive, so weigh whether or not purchasing branding items lines up with your business and conversion goals. Here are a few places you can go to order branding items, such as pens, coffee mugs, and totes:

» PromoDirect.com
» RushImprint.com
» EPromos.com
» InkHead.com
» Branders.com
» DiscountMugs.com
» Halo.com
» Customink.com
» 4imprint.com
» Lovelypackage.com

Lovelypackage.com is one of my favorite sites for exceptionally unique package design. This site will give you great ideas for standing out, no matter what you're selling. Remember, your product packaging should be functional, look amazing, reflect your brand, be cost effective, and reflect your typical customer.

> *Be so good they can't ignore you.*
> —STEVE MARTIN

Even if you don't have a product, you can still be creative with the way you conduct your service-based business. Colorful, creative paper products make everyone happy. Life's short. Be innovative and expressive with your branding materials. By doing so, you're not only doing your part to wipe bad business cards off the face of the earth, you're ensuring yours won't end up in the trash bin.

Public Speaking

Speaking is such a fun thing to do once you get over your fear of it. When people tell you to imagine everyone is naked to help you get over your jitters, ignore that advice. Just understand how much power you have at that moment. You have five hundred pairs of eyes focused directly on you and what you're selling (because really, as a speaker, you're selling something—an idea, a method, a thought process, a product, whatever). You have a captive audience that is there to listen to what you have to say for forty-five minutes. Bring your A game.

If you're compelling and provide something of value in your talk, you're going to win supporters. Don't be boring. Tell good jokes and be funny. At the same time, be serious and project your smartness in a non-prideful way. At that moment, you are an expert because someone hired you to speak. Clearly define what your audience can expect to get out of your talk and don't disappoint.

You can create a buzz about your services or products and possibly do back-of-the-room selling. If you're compelling enough, everyone will be dying to buy your product or service.

Haven't built your speaking business up enough to get paid to do it? Not a problem. Pay your teenager or a virtual assistant to research every small meeting group that pertains to your topic(s). Send them a great email offering to speak for free.

Chapter Twenty

OUT-OF-THE-BOX WAYS TO GROW YOUR BIZ

Old marketing is where you look for customers.
New marketing is where customers look for you.

Writing for SEO

There are standard ways to grow your business, but in our digital marketing age, there are ways to attract new customers that just weren't available a decade ago. Writing content with the specific purpose of SEO to bring in new clients or customers is one of those ways. It doesn't matter if you're a skilled writer. You probably took an English class in high school, and so that means you're a decent writer. You don't have any excuses.

Writing for SEO simply means you're producing content on your blog or website that's relevant to your business or your product. It doesn't have to be a thesis; your blog post can be simple yet powerful. Blog posts about lists are currently wildly popular, as is anything to do with providing insight into learning something new. The possibilities for content are endless. The hardest part is just parking your butt in your chair and cranking something out.

An easy way to find ideas for things to write about is to see what everyone else is talking about. BuzzSumo.com is an online tool that searches the web for the most shared content. Knowing this will help you come up with some sort of commentary. As an example, I just typed in "work smarter" into the BuzzSumo search bar. There are lots of list-type articles, such as "Work Smarter not Harder: 15 Great Tips" that has been shared over 30 thousand times. One article about how working abroad makes you smarter has been shared almost 100 thousand times. Using BuzzSumo or similar tools will help you determine what types of content will most likely do very well across all of the social platforms.

In addition to BuzzSumo, you can use Twitter's advanced search tool to see what's trending. Twitter is real time, so it's a great indicator of what's popular right now. You can ride the wave if you can pump out content fairly quickly. If you absolutely abhor writing, think about having your VA write articles for you or go to TextBroker.com or WritersAccesscom. You'll easily be able to find someone with writing experience in your specific niche.

Blogging is a free way to attract people who never would've found you. If you're sharing your original (some people use the word organic) content to all of the social media sites, aim to bring people back to your site. You'll need to make sure you create a cool graphic for your blog post with tools such as Quozio.com, or find one using the Creative Commons search tool (search.creativecommons.org). It's pointless to share a blog post without a picture when a compelling picture with text overlay is usually what converts in the first place.

If you can write for someone who has a larger audience than you, then you'll fare even better. I have a few friends who write humor. Every once in a while, they submit their posts to other blogs with very high traffic. When their blog posts are accepted, they get upwards of ninety thousand hits on their blogs because of the exposure. They end up selling a lot of their books from their own websites. It's totally worth their time to write for other blogs because of the big payoff.

> $mart Tip: Use an editorial calendar to stay on top of blog posts. Try to schedule one a week in the beginning, so as not to become overloaded. Once blogging becomes easier, try posting two or more times a week.

Create Exclusivity

Exclusivity breeds excitement. I don't know about you, but when I was in high school and heard about a private party someone was having, I wanted in. It's in our DNA to crave what we can't have, and the same principle works in your marketing strategies. Creating an invite-only group will make those you invited feel important, and those who aren't in the group will want in once they hear about it. I'm in a few super-secret social media groups, and for whatever reason, I just love the idea of that. It's so covert and cool.

You can do a few things to create an exclusive group. Before your new business launches, you can let your sphere know you're creating a by-invitation-only LinkedIn or Facebook group where you're going to share helpful and cutting-edge information that will change their lives forever. Something like that. Then send them a nice email using MailChimp or other trackable web-based email service. In the body of the email, explain what the group will be about and make sure you emphasize that it's by invitation only and that the initial amount of people allowed in will be limited.

Once those in your sphere opt in, give them what you promised. Don't spam them every day, but be strategic in giving them a great piece of information a few times a week. If you help other people, then they will want to help you. For the most part, people feel good about sharing content from those whom they like and trust. If you are always being generous with providing resources to others, when it comes time for you to ask something of them, they'll be glad to oblige.

Here's how to start a Facebook group: https://www.facebook.com/help/167970719931213, and here's how to start your own LinkedIn group: https://help.linkedin.com/app/answers/detail/a_id/1164/kw/create+a+group.

MeetUp

A great way to meet new people you otherwise would never have met is to create a MeetUp group. According to Quora, MeetUp has 8 million members in a hundred countries, and 50k MeetUps are scheduled every week. Users on MeetUp scour the site to find things to do in their area and to find others with shared interests.

As an organizer of a group, you'll have to pay monthly or yearly fees, but MeetUp has a free trial period so you can feel it out and see if it's something that you like doing. In my area, it is around $80 a year to host a MeetUp group. MeetUp is very organized in that you create a profile for your group with specific intent. MeetUp will then show your group to users who've identified that they are interested in the topics your MeetUp is all about.

For instance, I started a MeetUp group centered around social media tips and tricks. I created a catchy image banner and listed in detail all of the things I hoped the MeetUp group would provide to others. Once the group went public, I had over one hundred people join the group in a matter of a day or two. Then, I scheduled

MeetUps at local free venues, such as libraries and credit unions with conference rooms, where I taught classes for free. It was a great way to get my name out in the community, and I made a lot of contacts.

MeetUps can charge members fees to come to events or the events can be free; it's the organizer's choice how the group is set up. My group was free, but I'm in a wine appreciation group that charges a five-dollar fee to attend meetings to cover the cost of the organizer's time. And I'm totally okay with paying that.

Check out MeetUp and consider whether or not you might be able to subtly integrate it into your marketing plan. There are so many people looking to connect with others who share the same interests. I'm sure you'll find a niche there and rock it. Visit http://help.meetup.com to get started.

Book Clubs

Never be afraid to do something new. Remember, amateurs built the ark; professionals built the Titanic.
—UNKNOWN

I have a friend who owns a mortgage broker-age. She's such a creative marketer, and I'm blown away by all of the marketing strate-gies she implements, which is why she's the top broker around here. One of the things she does is host a book club for Realtors®. There are a lots of benefits to this strategy, the biggest one being she's creating relationships with the people who can keep her business going. Secondarily, she's building rapport and relationships within her community by bringing people together to share a common interest: reading.

She develops a list at the beginning of the year of trending busi-ness books that she feels will add value to someone's life. All of the books she chooses are fantastic and bring value to the reader. The book club meets once a month at a public venue to discuss the book, and sometimes not everyone has finished or even read the book.

My friend is building her business with strategies that are atypical but work because she realizes marketing means relationship building.

Do you have time to read one book a month? If so, consider putting together a book club in your area, specific to your business. You can develop relationships with those whom you might not have access to any other way. Go to Goodreads.com and type in the search bar "business books" or "popular books (and the year)." You'll find tons of lists to start building a great book club.

Teaching for Free

Giving of your time might sound counterintuitive when you're trying to start a business. Trust me, you're going to do a lot of it in the beginning, and it's okay. Teaching and speaking for free is one way to quickly get in front of a whole bunch of people and make connections. The only thing that it costs you is your time. Aside from teaching within a MeetUp group you created, consider all of the other local groups you could teach something to.

Ask your sphere what groups they belong to and make a list. Go online and determine the best contact email address for each individual group and add it to your list. Send a personalized email to each group explaining what it is you do and why you're qualified to speak or teach something to their group. If you can provide value to the group, more than likely they'll let you come in to teach. Use the opportunity to brand yourself or your business as the local expert. Hand out your business cards and ask the audience for their email addresses so they can receive more great content from you or be notified of sales, giveaways, etc.

A while back, I spoke to a great group of women over fifty. They were lively and eager to learn. And lots of them were businesses owners or related to someone who owned a business. I got tons of great referrals from the group, and it only cost me an hour and a half of my time. They even paid for my lunch! It was a great experience for everyone involved.

There are so many different organizations and groups within communities. I'm sure you'll easily be able to find a few. Simply type in "networking groups" plus your city into Google, and a few groups will pop up. MeetUp has tons of groups, so check there too. Ask your local business center for referrals for groups that meet in your area. There are also groups affiliated with AARP, Kiwanas, and MOPS (Moms need stimulation too, you know, and some of them are married to someone who owns a business).

Volunteer for Committees and Boards

Volunteering on local and national boards can take a lot of your time. Many times, board members are not paid for their services. Offering up your time can be hard when you're trying to start a business, so you might want to make sure you're ready to commit to a board or wait until your business is running somewhat smoothly before you decide to volunteer. The benefits of volunteering can far outweigh the time spent.

I volunteer on a few committees and one board. The board is for a local writing group that supports writers and promotes literacy and the arts within our community. It's an unpaid position but has many perks. I get to meet some amazing people I would never have met had I not volunteered for the board. I'm making a difference in my community (even if it's a small one), and in serving others, I'm helping myself in so many ways.

I've gotten a lot of business just by being a part of this group. I've also been introduced to *NY Times* best-selling authors and was able to have an intimate dinner with a Pulitzer Prize winner. I was on cloud nine for at least a month. I have a picture with that man on my desktop, reminding me that serving others can connect me to my dreams, and it can do the same thing for you.

Think about ways you can serve others in your community. Keep your eye out for volunteer opportunities and never pass up a chance to pour out into others. You never know what the end result will be.

Host Events

I have tons of kids and don't have a lot of time for other things. My family is my first priority, and that's the way I've designed my life. I have no problem telling a person no when asked to do something that takes time away from the things I deem important. If I want to do something, I have to figure out something else to cut out of my life or I have to sleep less. Every time I come home with a new idea, my husband worries it translates into him having to purchase more bags of coffee beans from Costco than usual.

Someday I'm sure I'll have less energy, but until then, I'll carry on as usual. I have an attitude of living and loving big, and it's contagious. Because of this, I end up hosting a few really large events within my community related to non-profits. These events take an immense amount of planning and execution, but the payoff is the visibility I have within the community. I don't do it just for that, but it's a natural benefit.

When you're a part of something big, you meet big thinkers and community thought and action leaders. You want these people in your sphere because these are the people you want in your corner rooting for you. Large events bring community together and give everyone a common goal. The end result is a sense of purpose and satisfaction, which in turn will end up interweaving you together. Consider volunteering or hosting a large community event. Give it a try just once and see what great things come from it.

Podcasting

Podcasting is another way to reach a huge audience in an unconventional way. Top podcasting coach Kris Gilbertson says in her book *Podcasting for Promotion, Positioning & Profit*, by podcasting, "You're reaching an affluent, hard to reach, highly desirable target market."

You can use free tools like Audacity editor to create your podcast, and you'll need a good microphone that plugs into your USB port on your computer or laptop. I have a Yeti Blue and love the sound quality. You'll need to pay for a site that hosts and stores your online media. If you use a provider like Libsyn to store your online media, you can add a tab directly on your Facebook page showcasing your Podcast: https://www.facebook.com/libsynapp.

To learn how to make a podcast, visit: https://www.apple.com/itunes/podcasts/specs.html.

While iTunes is the most common place to upload your podcast, also consider Stitcher.com and TuneIn.com (Amazon's Alexa device streams TuneIn to its listeners).

Podcasting helps promote your platform, but it can also just be a lot of fun to do one. I have a humor podcast with *NY Times* best seller AK Turner to balance my left brain. It's really fun to hear from listeners from all over the planet, and it's a great way for others to feel personally connected to you. Search for the *Tales of Imperfection* podcast within iTunes if you'd like to get to know me aside from the content in this book.

Email Signature

Sometimes it's the subtle things that can make all the difference. A long time ago, someone sent me an email with clickable links to their social media sites. This was before social media was super popular. I was surprised (and impressed) at how many social media sites this person was on, and I easily connected with them simply because they listed all of the sites underneath their name within their email to me. Nothing screamed, "Like my pages!" or "Buy my crap right now!"

Creative marketing means trying almost everything and measuring what works. It's so easy to create an email signature, and once you do, you don't have to change it again unless you close down one of your websites or social media platforms. The more colorful and exciting you make it, the more likely someone is going to click on it. Just make sure if you go back and forth in an email thread you don't keep including your signature. It can make scrolling through the thread harder and cause frustration.

Here's a resource to create a free email signature: Wisestamp.com.

Create an Online Magazine

A creative and unique way to reach an untapped market is to create an online magazine. It can be a collaborative effort if you have found people with a vision similar to yours. Within my community, we have a few collaborative online magazines produced and edited by small business owners and solopreneurs.

Electronic publishing is time consuming, but it doesn't cost you anything but time. You'll end up with an amazing digital product that's shareable internationally. Digital publishing does have a learning curve, but it's not as steep as you might think. And as usual, you can hire it out if you don't want to do it yourself. An online magazine creates an image of professionalism and can set you apart from your competitors. You can embed the magazine right onto your website using simple WordPress plugins.

Check out Joomag.com and ISSUU.com to discover the benefits of online publishing.

Write an eBook

If you can actually sit your butt in your desk chair for 120 hours and finish an eBook, you're ahead of the curve and deserve the accolades of a published author. A print book is much harder to produce than an eBook, so start with an eBook if writing a book is on your to-do list. Having a book under your belt helps you build your platform and can distinguish you from your competitors. It's hard to complete a book but not impossible. A book is a great way to increase your credibility, which will in turn result in more sales and income for you. Not sure where to start? Here are a few places to learn about the eBook industry and ways to publish a book:

» Smashwords.com
» BookBaby.com
» IngramSpark.com
» CreateSpace.com

No matter what, please pay someone to design a professional cover for your book and hire an editor. You'll give all of us other authors a bad name if you don't put reasonable effort and expense into producing a professional product. If you're wondering, Derek at CreativIndie.com produced my cover.

Chapter Twenty-One

HOW TO HANDLE GROWTH: CLIENT MANAGEMENT

Goals are meant to be reached, and numbers are meant to be broken.

Customer Relationship Management (CRM) Software

Customer relationship management (CRM) software helps ensure clients don't slip through the cracks. The most popular CRMs offer sales, marketing, invoicing, recruiting, and service management to businesses of all sizes. Some of them have extra benefits like Facebook, Twitter, and LinkedIn integrations and can capture leads and offer an online storefront.

Applications such as Contactually.com help you maximize ROI by telling you when and with whom you should be keeping in touch. Here are some client relationship management systems to check out:

» Infusionsoft.com
» SageCRM.com

- » Salesforce.com
- » Zoho.com/CRM
- » Nimble.com
- » Insightly.com
- » SugarCRM.com
- » HighRiseHQ.com

RingCentral

RingCentral is a cloud-based phone and fax system for businesses. You can easily secure a 1-800 or 1-888 toll-free phone number with extensions and an automated answering service. When callers dial in, they will hear a customized message from you and be given choices based on parameters that you've pre-determined. This service gives you a professional answering service without having to pay the big bucks.

When someone calls my 1-888 RingCentral number, I'll see the incoming call on my desktop or smartphone, depending on how I have it set up. If I don't take the call, it'll go to voicemail, and RingCentral will alert me via email and within my smartphone app that I've missed a call and have a message. I can then listen to the message from my desktop or phone and return the call using either of those options.

RingCentral also has a cloud faxing service, which is so convenient sometimes. All I have to do is scan a document from my computer, and I can send it as a fax via RingCentral from my desktop or mobile device. Faxing is still necessary sometimes, and it's oh-so-nice to have that capability at my fingertips.

RingCentral has monthly plans based on your needs, and you can usually negotiate a lower fee if you pay for a year in advance. RingCentral will become an integral part of your business. Check it out by visiting RingCentral.com.

Chapter Twenty-Two

THE 9-TO-5 ESCAPE ARTIST ATTITUDE

Greet the dawn with enthusiasm, and you
may expect satisfaction by sunset.
—AMISH PROVERB

Think about the happiest, most successful people in your sphere. Who has the best attitude? Who has the best relationships? Who is the most balanced? Granted, we don't know what goes on in secret, but for the most part, it's easy to identify those who have attained mastery in certain areas.

Wake up every morning and give yourself five minutes of reflection. This will clear your mind, focus your thoughts, and get you ready to live the day with gratitude. Just sucking down air should make you feel happy because it means you're still alive. We 9-to-5 escape artists are blessed people. If you're successful at the 9-to-5 escape, then you're living the life you want to live. You've designed every day to be the way you want it, and you're living life to full capacity.

The 9-to-5 escape artist attitude is one of controlled optimism and hope. The world needs successful people to lead and encourage others to reach for the stars. If you're reading this book, the fire inside of you won't stop burning until you quench it with action. And even then, it will only become a controlled burn. When you look at every day as an opportunity to live to your strengths, and you're doing what you want to do, you will go to bed with peace and contentment.

Be a Leader

Many of us wanted to be the president when we were little. Then reality set in, and we discovered not everyone can become the leader of the free world. I personally wouldn't want to deal with all

> *You cannot get through a single day without having an impact on the world around you. What you do makes a difference, and you have to decide what kind of difference you want to make.*
> —JANE GOODALL

of that crap anyway. But you're a leader in your own right. We all have a strain of leadership within us. Leaders are not born; leaders are made.

Your background is not indicative of your leadership potential. You simply have to have a vision and know how to guide others into your thought processes. 9-to-5 escape artists are usually visionaries. They see potential in almost everything and know how to turn their vision into something that produces real dollars. Thought leaders emerge when an idea takes hold and catches on.

9-to-5 escape artists can change lives. I'm serious! They can breathe life into someone who is unsatisfied with life and sees no alternative to what they already have. Once you start living the 9-to-5 escape artist lifestyle, don't keep it a secret. Become the town crier and share it from the rooftops. Your sphere needs your thought leadership. Your story can be the catalyst for someone else to completely remodel their lives and the lives of their children.

Be the change you want to see. You have no idea how many lives you might help redesign for the better.

Your background is not indicative of your leadership potential.

Be an Activator

Activators change the world! If you aren't one, you probably already know it subconsciously. You're not an activator if even reading the words *take action now* scares you. You need to acquire activator skills, or it's time to bring in a partner who's an activator. They will be the brawn to your brain (plus they'll be smart too, so it'll be like you have two brains).

A word of caution: choose carefully. There is a difference between an activator and a smooth operator. Activators talk and act and can convince others to take action. In fact, they have a weird way of making you think there's no choice other than to get moving. On the other hand, smooth operators' schmoozes can be manipulative. They are experts at talking people into doing things, but then they lack the standards, drive, or tools to follow through with the implementation phase.

Make sure you thoroughly profile a potential business partner. Who cares if you make them take three personality tests? If they don't like it, then they don't have the stamina to be a great partner anyway.

Characteristics of Thriving 9-to-5 Escape Artists

Working for someone else can actually be a great motivator to start your own business. I strategically encouraged my teen girls to get a job the moment they were legally able to work. I knew if they didn't know how the system works, then they wouldn't understand how to challenge it in a good way. I love the discussions we have after they've worked a five-hour shift, realizing after taxes they probably netted $30. When they're used to getting an $80 pair of jeans using my money, it's not as valuable to them. But when they have to work for the money and pay for the jeans on their own, the value of money shifts. If you're a parent, giving your teen money without them having to earn it will ensure a warped concept of entitlement. My teens are already strategizing how they can leverage their time to make more money. They've come up with some hair-brained ideas and a few very good ones. I always encourage these strategy sessions, even though they don't know that's the term for what we're doing.

When a 9-to-5 escape artist lifestyle comes up in discussion, most people will say "I really want to do this," but doing something and saying you're going to do something brings about different results. Talking is great. Planning is smart. But what's the point if you're missing the implementation? You'll never *find* the time to accomplish your dreams; you have to *make* the time. Just as this book didn't write itself, I would've never gotten it accomplished had I not diligently scheduled the time to get it done.

If you believe becoming a 9-to-5 escape artist will change your life for the better, and you believe you can make the world a better place with your talents or ideas, you're already on the right path to successful lifestyle design.

Characteristics of thriving 9-to-5 escape artists include:
- » Innovative and willing to try a new tactic even if no one has done it before
- » Voracious learners and readers
- » Teachable
- » Uses time wisely and doesn't waste it

» Leaders, encouragers, willing to reject the status quo and challenge it

Ask for Help When You Need It

Sometimes we are weak in certain areas during changing seasons of life or illness. If you're a new parent, you know what I'm talking about. Newborns and sleep do not go hand-in-hand. I pretty much needed to clone my real self when my third child was born because a crazy, sleep-deprived person posing as me was doing things that I certainly would not be doing in my right mind.

Our prime purpose in this life is to help others. And if you can't help them, at least don't hurt them.
—DALI LAMA

I am not proud of my 9-to-5 escape artist self at that time, and I'm so thankful my clients stuck it out with me. If I did something evil to you during that time, this is a blanket public apology that whatever happened is not an indication of my true self.

I even got two speeding tickets in the same week, one of them on Valentine's Day of all days. I did not show any love to the police officer, nor he to me. From my experience, I believe police officers should be trained in sleep deprivation versus intoxication. I explained to them I was just trying to hurry home so I could sleep, but I guess everyone says that—or that their kid has to pee.

The no-sleep thing went on for a *long time* because, unbeknownst to me, I had a child with Sensory Processing Disorder. Apparently the universe decided I was the perfect candidate for a child who cried all the time and didn't need to sleep.

So, I needed help! Lots of help. I knew it. My husband knew it. I used to have a problem asking for help. "I can do it myself," I'd lie to myself. "No one can do it as well as I can." Another big lie. I'd pride myself on how much I could do, when I really shouldn't have been doing it. When you daydream about your sheets, it should be your first clue there's a problem.

Now I have no problem asking for help. I think seeing my unmatched earrings and half-braided hair scared my work buddies into action. My colleagues came alongside me and managed my insurance book of business, and my realtor friends stepped up and watched my real estate investments for me.

Not asking for help when you really need it is dumb and slightly prideful. Those who recognize there's a fire in the house before the house burns down are the wiser for it.

Know Your Weaknesses

Knowing your weaknesses can be just as helpful as knowing your strengths. I'm an opportunity seeker, and a weakness of mine is

> *To share your weakness is to make yourself vulnerable; to make yourself vulnerable is to show your strength.*
> —CRISS JAMI

menial organizational tasks. (I'm not a small details person. Who cares about the small stuff? I'm on a mission to change the world!)

But those receipts strewn all over my desk don't file themselves, so what's a 9-to-5 escape artist lacking filing skills to do? Obviously, I'd better get help or I'll have a problem. I could engage receipt-filing services from my teens as a punishment for always missing curfew, but the smarter idea would be to hand everything over to our IRS-rule-following-to-the-letter CPA.

If I'm awful at something like sorting and filing, recognizing it and then finding someone who's a ninja master at filing random pieces of paper will serve me well and end up making my business more profitable.

I also know I'm weak in the area of saying no. Well, that's not entirely true. I can easily say no to working in our church's childcare nursery or to my teens when they want to buy hundred-dollar designer bedazzled jeans. I have a really hard time saying no when an acquaintance asks me to look at their business plan or a friend needs me to critique their website or a random person at a conference I'm speaking at asks me if I have a few minutes to expand on the current marketing trends.

Write down areas where you know you are weak and either hire someone to fill the gap or trade services with someone you trust and can depend on. Done and done!

Forge Ahead

Successful 9-to-5 escape artists do not allow life to get in the way; they make life the way they want it.

When you experience a setback that isn't severe, it's not too difficult to shift your thoughts and feelings from negative into positive ones. Usually little setbacks are nothing more than small annoyances. But when you get handed a doozy, if you're not prepared, you can go into a tailspin.

If you lose a client that provided 40 percent of your income, you'll probably freak out. If one of your key managers leaves without notice and takes a few major clients with him, you might have a tough time leaving for a pre-planned trip to Disneyland. If you find out an employee is embezzling money when she was supposed to be putting the money toward payroll taxes, you'll probably temporarily become best friends with the bottle of premium tequila your favorite client just gave you. But the bottom line is that you won't die. Do not fear what will come in the day. No matter what happens, you must do what the famous book says and feel the fear and do it anyway. Just take a breath, take action to conquer the problem at hand, and overcome. Successful 9-to-5 escape artists do not allow life to get in the way; they make life the way they want it.

Chapter Twenty-Three

HOW DOES SHE KNOW SO MUCH?

When it comes to information, there are two camps. One camp says we're exposed to too much information and we don't need it. This camp encourages the application of filters and believes ignorance is bliss. The other camp feels that information is power and you should access it at the speed of light and assimilate as much of it as possible. Maybe there's also a camp positioned in the middle that waffles back and forth between the other two camps. Whether by choice or by necessity, you fall into one of these categories.

I'm in the camp that feels having lots of information equals a superior advantage. I wouldn't know most of the things I do if I hadn't gleaned information from books, periodicals, blogs, tweets, and everything else. Of course, you can experience information overload, so you have to identify what you want to learn and read about and how you'll receive the information.

Talkwalker alerts are a great way to get email notifications regarding topics you're interested in (talkwalker.com/alerts). You'll get an email delivered to your inbox whenever something is on the Internet that meets the parameters you've set within Talkwalker. It's similar to Google alerts and can be customized to your tastes.

I even suggest putting your name, your business name, and your kids' names into these systems so you can monitor things that are being said about you online.

I use Zinio.com and NextIssue.com to easily read and store all of my current magazines. I love the fact that I can pay $15 a month to NextIssue and have access to all of the most popular magazines on the market. When I'm waiting in the carpool line to pick up my kid, I can quickly consume a magazine or two directly from my iPad.

I also am in love with my Flipboard app (Flipboard.com). Within Flipboard you can bring in all of your favorite websites, blogs, and social platforms and view all new posts and activity in a beautiful magazine-style spread. You "flip" through posts just as you would flip through a magazine. It's so much fun and can be an easy way to stay on top of information.

BlogLovin.com is also one of my favorite ways to stay on top of blogs. Sometimes I don't have time to flip through Flipboard, and I like that BlogLovin will send me an email with updates on blog posts I missed. I can quickly skim through the email and click on an article that looks appealing.

I agree with those who believe that you must have moderation in everything. If you spend too much time researching and reading, then you're not spending enough time taking action. It's important to design your life in a way that it all balances. I suggest pulling out your calendar and scheduling at least one hour of reading time a day. When the timer's up, then stop. Guard this time fiercely and do not allow for interruptions. This strategy will ensure you get adequate reading time so that you feel like you're giving yourself enough brain food to stay on top of your game.

I blame my mother, in a good way, for my incessant desire to devour books. As a child, I remember her taking me to the library each week. She'd run her fingers over the new releases as if they were the rarest and finest creations on planet Earth. When I was not behaving, my punishment was the removal of my books or not being able to visit the library. What she did (without knowing it) was create in me the value and desire to consume books at the subconscious level.

Later, in the nineties, she introduced me to rudimentary software she'd found somewhere to train an individual to read faster. I'd watch a ball bounce from corner to corner on the computer screen with the objective to train my eyes to move faster and more efficiently. My words-per-minute reading number increased substantially, and in turn my mother created a monster. Instead of once a week, I began to ask to visit the library three times a week. If the Kindle had been invented at that time, my mother would have saved a lot of gas, and I would've ended up an Amazon Top 100 reviewer. It's never too late to train yourself to be a better reader.

Try this app that measures how fast you read and helps you read faster: www.spritzlet.com. You can also add it to your bookmarks in your browser and read articles and pages faster than you normally would.

Sometimes speed-reading reduces your comprehension, so don't focus so much on hitting a certain reading speed as trying to read more content than usual. The goal is to increase consumption of text so your brain gradually increases the rate at which it processes information. Your retina is only able to move as fast as it was designed, so don't try to go all Terminator on your reading. Just for fun, check out this article on the different speed-reading techniques and the science behind them: http://lifehacker.com/the-truth-about-speed-reading-1542508398.

Another good read is by Ryan Battles: https://ryanbattles.com/post/how-to-become-a-faster-reader.

Let's face it: sometimes you're born with a high IQ, and sometimes, like me, you have to download information into your brain to catch up with all of the brainiacs out there. No matter what your intelligence level, the fact of the matter is that readers are smarty-pants. The average US citizen reads only five books a year.[12] If you read one book per week, think about how much more you'll know than the average person. This will serve you well when running your business.

With the advent of Audible and the Kindle "Read to Me" function, there's no reason you can't download a few books into your brain every month. My car has Bluetooth in it. When I'm dropping the kids off, I'm either listening to an instructional podcast or I'm listening to a book. When I can talk myself into getting to the gym, I'm listening there too. When I have to do those mundane things that I hate, like changing the litter box, I'm learning from a *NY Times* best seller while I'm scooping crap.

---

12 Source:
www.pewinternet.org/2014/01/16/a-snapshot-of-reading-in-america-in-2013/

Chapter Twenty-Four

SUCCESS IS CONTAGIOUS

Walk with the dreamers, the believers, the courageous, the cheerful, the planners, the doers, the successful people with their heads in the clouds and their feet on the ground.
—WILFRED PETERSON

According to the famous motivational speaker Jim Rohn, you are the average of the five people you spend the most time with. You assimilate their thoughts, beliefs, mannerisms, and mind-sets. If you're trying to build and maintain a positive sense of self and a strong business, you're going to have to pick those five people carefully and strategically. Not that you want to have friends only because you get something from them, but you need to be mindful of what you're getting out of relationships when you spend time with people.

I definitely have expectations for my relationships, because my time here on earth is limited. Most of my inner circle knows they're in my circle of trust because they've proven themselves trustworthy, a very important characteristic for me. I don't want to waste time with people who don't have my best interests at heart and aren't good for me or for my lifestyle aspirations. So, yes, I qualify my friends and my close business relationships.

I give people a little piece of me and see if they can be good stewards with the tiny bit I give them. If so, then I'll give them more. For example, I'll tell someone a small detail of something that I'm working on and finish the statement with, "Very few people know about this, so I'd like to keep it between you and me." Then I'll wait. If someone else in my sphere knows about it and mentions something to me or I hear questions from someone else, I'll know the first person I was qualifying talks too much or doesn't value my requests as I would like them to. I will then categorize them accordingly. Alternatively, if someone doesn't do the aforementioned, then I'll mentally put them into the get-to-know-better category.

We all put our friends into certain groups. I have my work friends, friends who are always ready to go out and have fun, friends who'll drop everything to watch my kids even though they have four kids, shopping girlfriends, creative friends, my writing friends ... you get the idea. I tend to call up friends based on where I've categorized them and what our common interests are. If I have an amazing business idea, I probably won't call my shopping friends or my playgroup friends. This is why I really love Google+. You can put people in "circles" and notify them about things you know will interest them. I've put everyone I know into my Google+ circles so I can make sure I don't miss anyone and can keep up with our common interests.

Once upon a time, I had a friend who started turning into a jealous witch (but substitute the w for a b). These people are usually like this at their core, but I hadn't identified it because we hadn't been in a

> *It's hard to soar like an eagle when you are surrounded by turkeys.*
> —UNKNOWN

situation where we'd been in the same playing field, and it hadn't manifested yet. We became involved in a fun local non-profit group. After a while, I was invited to be the coordinator for the group's events in my city, and this person became snide about it.

After reading the *War of Art* by Steven Pressfield, I realized she was most certainly a blocked creative. She brought me down, was rude, and was never uplifting. Passive-aggressive statements toward me became the norm. Questions like, "Are you sure you're supposed to do it that way?" were meant to cause doubt and take the joy from what I was doing. I recognized her attitude was that of a blocked creative and reached out to her, but I received no response.

This is your first clue you've identified the problem—when someone doesn't respond to you. They don't want to acknowledge the problem and are scared because you've identified it before they have. The bottom line is that sometimes you need to cut ties because a relationship isn't bringing anything positive into your life, and it has the potential to do more harm than good.

If you have any limiting beliefs, it's important to identify where you're getting them from. If someone in your life is speaking negatively to you about your goals and desires, then you need to pull them out of your life just as quickly as you would a tick burrowing in your dog. Just as Lyme disease can be prevented by scanning and checking for ticks, so too should you periodically check for those who are trying to infiltrate your no-limiting beliefs thinking style. The smallest of creatures can create full-body damage if you don't catch it in time. Family is the exception. You can't cut them out of your life; you simply have to cut them off if and when their dream-killing statements begin.

My favorite individuals are those I call connectors. These are the people whose primary goal when it comes to relationships is to connect someone to something or someone else, their core belief being that everyone is better for it. When you find one of these people, be grateful for them. If I have a need within one of my businesses, I'll simply send out a request to the handful of people who I believe are my primary connectors. I try to help them out whenever they have a request for where to find information or how to get something they need, and they do the same for me. These people are highly important to me and are at the extreme opposite of those I categorize as time wasters.

Guard your time as you guard your daughter's virginity. You must be hyper-aware of those who might seek to steal your time. I get a lot of LinkedIn requests from people I don't know who ask to have coffee with me so we can see if we can mutually help each other. Kudos to them for trying, but if I had a coffee meeting with everyone who felt we could mutually benefit each other, I'd have a heart attack from the caffeine overdose. If you haven't already, read the amazing book by Bob Beaudine titled *The Power of Who: You Already Know Everyone You Need to Know.* You do. I promise.

Chapter Twenty-Five

LIVE YOUR BEST LIFE

Drop the idea that you are Atlas carrying the world on your shoulders. The world would go on even without you. Don't take yourself so seriously.
—NORMAN VINCENT PEALE

Newsflash: the world keeps moving when we screw up. And if everything goes to crap, your attitude might be the only thing you have control over. So don't take yourself too seriously.

As a 9-to-5 escape artist, you're a thought and change leader. Americans are entirely too anxious, too stressed out, and too worried about one-upping their neighbor. We need to be the change we want to see in our country. It starts with an idea, and then the idea turns into a movement. Remind yourself how thankful you are for the time you do have. You never know what day will be your last, so just roll with whatever comes your way. Live your best life and encourage others to do the same.

Reach for the Stars (and Be Patient Along the Way)

Sometimes good things take a little time. It's going to take time to set up your business and the appropriate systems you'll need to start generating a nice income. Don't get discouraged, and don't give up. If you chip away at your goal every single day, you'll get there. I promise.

Some days will be bet-ter than others. But that's the same for everyone. If you begin

Even miracles take a little time.
—FAIRY GODMOTHER IN CINDERELLA

with the end goal in mind, then every action you take gets you one step closer to your goal. Never give up on your dreams. Ever. Your desires are burning inside of you because they're meant to be. If you stop working on your dreams, they'll still be inside you, burn-ing from the inside out.

Consider the story of J. K. Rowling, who was so poor she wasn't able to photocopy her first 90k-word fiction manuscript. She had to type out each version to send to publishers. We all know how wealthy she is today because of the *Harry Potter* series. Justin Bieber's single mother could barely afford to feed them both, and he'd play his guitar for extra money. He uploaded videos of himself to YouTube and was brought on the *Ellen* show. Now he's one of the richest entertainers on the planet. Oprah Winfrey suffered child-hood trauma but pursued her education and worked her way up the ranks on television. She never gave in or gave up, and she's now one of the top female earners in the world. If these once ordinary people can become extraordinary, so can you.

Learn to Adapt

Some people naturally roll with the punches, and some just don't. I'm a fairly easygoing person. My Autistic daughter is a little more rigid in the way she likes things, which is to be expected. My two teens like change now and then, and my husband has to be coaxed. He grew up in a household that didn't experience any change of patterns until his dad died when my husband was seventeen.

Sometimes life forces change, and we have to adapt. Other times, we choose to adapt to life because we recognize it will go better for us if we do. As 9-to-5 escape artists, it's really important to learn to adapt. If you haven't figured it out yet, life does not go as planned. Even with the best planning and with strategic implementation, things can go wrong or not as initially projected. I think pessimistic people call it Murphy's Law. I call it life.

> *The stiffest tree is most easily cracked, while bamboo or willow survives by bending in the wind.*
> —BRUCE LEE

Here's the deal, if you can easily adapt, you'll be happier all the way around. There's nothing worse than being around someone who freaks out when things don't go the way they'd like them to. Don't be one of those people.

Have you ever made dinner plans and then found out the restaurant is closed for a private party? Unless you live in a town with a population of one hundred, there are probably other options out there, and it's not worth getting upset over. Did someone close to you steal one of your ideas? You don't need to hire someone to break their legs. It'll be okay. And remember: as a 9-to-5 escape artist, you're supposed to avoid jail. Did your secretary steal from you? Maybe now you can hire that virtual assistant you've been wanting for a long time—the one you didn't hire because you felt bad about letting your secretary go. That secretary actually did you a favor.

If you look at life's setbacks as stepping-stones that are actually helping you get closer to your goal, you'll sleep much better at night. When you have setbacks or fail at something, you're learning something you wouldn't have learned otherwise. Growth usually comes during trials and difficult seasons in life. The wisest people I know are those who have suffered a setback. When you overcome a setback, you're gaining a new skill set.

Don't give up or give in when you're handed a challenge, even if it seems insurmountable. I am not a Darwin proponent, but I do like his statement that, "It's not the biggest, the brightest, or the best that will survive but those who adapt the quickest." Obviously, all the way back to cavemen, humans have adapted and survived. They didn't view the great beasts before them and say to themselves, "We're screwed, let's just give up now." Life goes on because we adapt, by choice or by force. It's easier if we choose to do it with purposeful intention, and a good attitude helps too.

Relationships Are the Currency of Life

Lifestyle design and being a 9-to-5 escape artist is all about relationships. If you have a million dollars in the bank but don't have any friends or family to share it with, you're going to be the most miserable millionaire on the planet. Your business and income goals should always rotate around your relationship goals. Don't get so wrapped up in yourself, your dreams, or your work that you neglect those who matter the most.

A great way to measure whether or not you're in balance with work and relationships is to outright ask those closest to you. And don't get mad if you don't like what they have to say. Are they telling you that you're in front of your computer too much? Are you missing important milestones or events? Are you regularly having dates with your significant other and your friends?

I make a point to connect with those I care about. It's important to me to take the time to send birthday cards in the mail (you know, that box outside that someone stops at every day and puts paper in?). I have a list of those I really want to spend time with.

I have to schedule time for people on my calendar or I know I'll forget, and it'll be a month before I see them again. The great thing about online calendars is you can schedule an event to recur so you won't forget. I make sure to put my friends on my calendar and set a reminder to call them. I also set weekly reminders to have coffee or go to happy hour with my closest friends. Whether or not we're all able to get together is of no consequence. At least an attempt is being made.

The point of becoming a 9-to-5 escape artist is being able to live your life and enjoy your relationships. This is what distinguishes you from everyone else; you've decided life is too short to miss out on. Do whatever you have to do to ensure you're cultivating healthy relationships.

Helping Others

You can have everything in life you want, if you will just help other people get what they want.
—ZIG ZIGLAR

Helping others is a key component to ensure a productive and well-lived life. Self-focused intent may initially drive success, but it won't ultimately lead to happiness or long-term success. Don't just give your time; give away your money too. Not Monopoly money. Real dollars.

Christians call it tithing, Bill and Melinda Gates of the Gates Foundation call it "Getting the resources out to the poorest in the world," and Ted Turner just throws money out the window as if he's got a forest of money trees in his backyard (he recently gave $1 billion to the United Nations).

Don't spend time doing things to please people who don't matter. Take the resources you have and do something that makes a lasting difference in the lives of others. No matter how much money you have, there's a rock-solid principle that if you give 10 percent or more of your time or money, you'll always be living in abundance. Don't believe me? Test it. See what happens in your life when you part ways with your money for a selfless cause.

My personal favorites are organizations that help stop sex trafficking of women and children, both in the United States and internationally. Ten percent of the proceeds from this book will go to one of these organizations:

» Natalie Grant's Hope for Justice (hopeforjustice.org)
» Messenger International/Pearl Alliance (messengerinternational.org/get-involved/pearl-alliance/)

Chapter Twenty-Six

LIFE HACKS

Life hacking is a term used to identify a cutting-edge or creative ways that can help people save time and money and also sanity. Life hacks can help solve everyday problems more efficiently than the standard way of doing things.

If you search for life hacks on Pinterest or any other social media site, you might find hacks that are helpful but not necessarily geared toward business. A person could really spend all day just looking at all of the creative hacks someone has discovered. For instance, putting pancake mix in a ketchup bottle for no-mess pancake making is brilliant, but I'm not talking about hacks like that.

There are life hack tools that will make your business run better, but you need to be very specific when you're searching for them. As an aspiring 9-to-5 escape artist, you'll want to write out the tasks that cause you the most grief. Then, research apps or software tools that may be useful in tackling and conquering (or at least controlling) the problem.

Technology is moving very quickly, and sometimes it's hard to keep up with trends or even identify what shortcuts may or may not be useful. If you slowly implement even just a few life hacks into your daily routine, you'll begin to notice a subtle ripple effect in your productivity, resulting in operating at maximum proficiency and effectiveness.

The following are life hacks I use and recommend for successfully managing life:

»   **Activewords.com**: Reduce time writing repetitive sentences with this helpful software.

»   **PlantoEat.com**: A meal-planning calendar and automated grocery shopping list maker. I especially like how I can quickly copy an online recipe into Plan to Eat by simply providing the recipe link.

»   **Wunderlist**: (available as an app) The best to-do list app out there. You can sync it to all your devices, and share your lists with others.

»   **RescueTime.com**: Your computer usage will be monitored, and you will receive a productivity score.

»   **DayOne**: (available as an app) Absolutely one of my favorite life hacks, this journal app alerts me to type what I've done during the day that's noteworthy. I can also take a picture of myself or upload one from my smartphone and insert it into my digital journal. I can create a PDF of the journal or email some or all of the entries to other people.

»   **Hootsuite.com**: Auto-schedule your social media accounts and view all platforms at the same time within Hootsuite.

»   **EvernoteFood**: (available as an app) Many people know about Evernote, but with Evernote Food you can quickly pinpoint where you had a great meal and exactly what you ordered.

» **Free-Time**: (available as an app) This app finds free time within your calendar. You can share this information with others via email, text, or phone bumping.

» **InboxPause.com** (for Gmail): Put incoming email messages on hold so you won't be distracted.

» **Amazon Prime** (Amazon.com): Set up auto delivery for all of your non-perishable groceries, home furnace filters, dog food, and anything else you can think of. With Amazon Prime's free shipping service, you're saving your fuel and your time.

» **1Password**: (available as an app) Securely store and easily access your passwords.

» **Cozi.com**: Manage everyone in your family with their scheduled text alerts. If you need to remember an event or remind a family member of an upcoming appointment, you can schedule a reminder text to go out at a pre-selected time.

» **Timer+**: (available as an app) Use this timer to make sure you don't go over your allotted time for a meeting or a speech. You can run multiple timers at once. This app is extremely useful when you are meeting with a long-winded client. The beeper is very helpful!

Tracking Down Email Addresses

Sometimes you really want to contact someone via email, but you just can't track down their email address. Here's a way to locate an email address that isn't too time consuming. I wouldn't do this regularly, but it can come in handy when you want to pitch something to a high-level individual who may not publicly post their contact information.

First, you need to have a Gmail account and download the Rapportive plugin to import rich contact information within your Gmail platform (Rapportive.com).

Then watch this video:

YouTube.com/watch?v=bQnO6Yv9SnE&t=178 and download a copy of the Google doc located at Bitly.com/name2email as listed and designed by Rob Ousbey from Distilled.net (thanks for posting this on YouTube, Rob!).

This tool should be used with the utmost respect for others and not as a way to spam people. 9-to-5 escape artists use tools like this only when we have an amazing idea, business plan, or pitch and there's no other way to contact someone. Sometimes we've just got to utilize all of the resources at our disposal—without coming across as a stalker.

Chapter Twenty-Seven

LIFESTYLE BUILDING WITH A FAMILY

Some people are of the mind-set that once you have kids, the party stops. This group lives it up while they can because they believe once kids are part of the equation, the fun stops and the serious-ness begins. They believe once you have children, heaven forbid you take them on a three-month trip to Roatan or become expats in Mexico for nine months. They fear the children will lose their identity and not be able to catch up (conform) with their peers when they return. This school of thought frowns upon nomadic living and encourages continuity in all areas, including establish-ing a no-move policy once the children become school age.

Getting into the school district of choice becomes the par-ents' top priority. They believe only children sent to private and top charter schools beginning in kindergarten and finishing as twelfth-graders will be high-level thinkers and top wage earners. This group of parents is hyper-focused on the standard pathways of success as determined by the status quo.

9-to-5 escape artists have a different mind-set. We prefer expe-rience with knowledge versus just knowledge. I'll take someone with business and street smarts any day over someone with head knowledge but zero application. Children of 9-to-5 escape artists are compassionate because they've seen other children in second or third world countries. They don't just look at pictures of great monuments, they've been to them because their parents aren't location based.

There's a huge online community based on nomadic homeschooling and RV schooling. Check out some of the blogs. They're really fun to read! The RoadSchool Mom podcast (https://itunes.apple.com/us/podcast/road-school-moms/id854587085) is rated number five among all educational podcasts, so there's an obvious draw to learning about schooling children in a non-traditional way.

Here are a few places where you can get useful information to help with homeschooling or developing a hybrid-homeschool plan while traveling:

» U.S.-Sponsored Overseas Schools (State.gov/m/a/os)
» LessonPlanet.com
» K12.com
» Pinterest has thousands of ideas for unit studies while you're traveling with your kids. (A unit study means choosing one topic and combining different subjects to revolve around and tie into that topic.)

We 9-to-5 escape artists choose to defy the status quo because it doesn't work for us. Something in our very nature fights against mediocrity and working our asses off so someone else can achieve their goals. We have our own goals in mind. We wake up every day with the intention of creating our best lives because we have only one life, and it's with a pre-set amount of days. We don't know what that number is, and we want to exhaust every opportunity to live a good life. If you have a special circumstance, you are not excluded from these statements. In fact, just the opposite. If you've been given more obstacles than the average person, then the 9-to-5 escape artist lifestyle is right up your alley.

I've always gravitated toward lifestyle design and cultivating my work life around my family and play time. As previously mentioned, my third daughter has Autism. If I had to ask for as much time off from a 9-to-5 job as I've taken to shuttle my daughter to specialists, I'd be standing in line at the unemployment office. I can't even count how many days I've been homebound caring for my son who catches every virus that passes through his preschool doors. My fifteen-year-old's cheer coach seems especially bent on inconveniencing the parents of the cheerleaders, as she sadistically schedules practices at a location other than the school at 3:15 on alternative days from when my daughter goes for her electives.

Fortunately, in our house, both parents are ready and available 24/7 for any situation that arises within the household dynamic—both onsite and off. Having a flexible schedule also helps in the romance department. My husband and I can have a date during the day whenever we want to. People are tired at the end of the day, so it's fun to hang out when the general population is working in a cubicle.

If life hands you unexpected news, be encouraged that you can successfully design your work and business endeavors around it. Nothing is insurmountable, especially if you design life with purposeful intention around the needs and responsibilities that you owe to yourself and to others.

If you use the Internet to make money, and you want to live a nomadic lifestyle, here are some helpful sites and apps to help you successfully navigate through your decision to live it up with your family:

ACCOMMODATIONS:

- » Couchsurfing.com
- » Booking.com
- » Hostelbookers.com
- » Hostelworld.com
- » Hotels.com
- » Travelocity.com
- » Orbitz.com
- » BedandBreakfast.com

HOME EXCHANGE SITES:

- » HomeExhange.com
- » LoveHomeSwap.com
- » Knok.com
- » HomeForExchange.com
- » HomeLink-usa.org
- » Intervac-homeexchange.com
- » International Vacation Home Exchange (IVHE.com)

FLIGHTS/TRANSPORTATION

- » Skyscanner.net
- » Vayama.com
- » Momondo.com
- » Kayak.com
- » Orbitz.com
- » Cheap-oAir.com
- » Eurail.com
- » Statravel.com

THINGS TO DO WHILE LIVING SOMEWHERE ELSE:

» SpottedbyLocals.com
» MeetUp.com
» Eventbrite.com
» Eventful.com
» BrownPaperBag.com
» Groupon.com (choose your location)
» AmazonLocal.com (choose your location)
» CityMaps2Go (Offline map app in case Google Maps fails you. Search locations and streets without access to the Internet.) Download from iTunes or Google Play.
» Cultural immersion: Lonely Planet and Footprint guides
» TripAdvisor.com
» For travel planning, TripIt works offline and will save your booking information for hotels, cars, and flights. You can create itineraries and prevent unnecessary time loss due to disorganization.

AK Turner
9-to-5 escape artist

AK Turner knew that taking the leap to become a full-time writer was a gamble, but two years after doing so, she had two titles on the *New York Times* best sellers list. She had her dream job and a wonderful family, but something was missing. Turner and her husband had always enjoyed traveling but did less of it than they would have liked. There seemed to be many reasons not to travel, from finances to school schedules, until the couple realized that these issues were obstacles only if that's how they chose to see them. Using home exchanges and airline miles reduced the cost of living overseas for months at a time, and they explored various combinations of home schooling, online schooling, Montessori, and international schools to keep up with their children's educations. By implementing systems to facilitate remote working and the digital nomad lifestyle, Turner and her family have lived for months at a time in Mexico and Australia, and are soon headed to Brazil. With continued plans to explore the world for a few months every year, Turner and her family live a life that now has all of the pieces in place. You can visit AK at AKTurner.com.

Chapter Twenty-Eight

START NOW

The secret to getting ahead is getting started.
—MARK TWAIN

You can read all of the books on the planet and attend every available webinar about how to live a 9-to-5 escape artist's life, but in order to enact a change in your lifestyle, you have to actually make a change. I know it's easy for me to say, "You can do it!" because I'm a 9-to-5 escape artist. But that's exactly why I'm saying it. I did not come from money. My parents encouraged education, but I didn't receive a degree in business administration. I didn't have any formal training in startups, marketing, or 9-to-5 escape artist tactics. I learned everything I know now because I was in the trenches, partly by necessity and partly by choice. And you can learn how to do it too.

Now that you understand how to set up a business properly, how to market in this new and fast-paced digital age we live in, and how to think like a 9-to-5 escape artist, there's only one step left. You have to go now and be a 9-to-5 escape artist. I believe anyone has the capacity to change his or her life for the better. All you have to do is believe that you can and begin implementing some of the steps I've outlined in this book.

No more excuses. You now know far more than the average person and just enough to be dangerous. Stop thinking about doing it. Just put one foot in front of the other and keep moving forward, advancing every day toward living a life beyond your wildest expectations.

The first step toward getting somewhere is to decide that you're not going to stay where you are.

—J. P. MORGAN

GLOSSARY

Business Terms

AMORTIZE– To liquidate a debt, especially by periodic payments to the creditor; to write off a cost of an asset gradually.

AP– Account payable; a liability to a creditor, carried on open account, usually for purchases of goods and services.

AR– Account receivable; a claim against a debtor, carried on open account, normally limited to debts due from the sale of goods and services.

ASSET– Something an entity has acquired and has monetary value.

BALANCE SHEET– A condensed statement showing the financial status of an entity on a specific date (normally on the last day of an accounting period).

BOARD OF DIRECTORS– A governing body of an incorporated firm, usually its members are elected and has decision-making authority.

BOOTSTRAPPING– Building a business out of very little or absolutely nothing. Usually a cash-only approach is implemented out of necessity.

CAPITAL– Money invested in a business to generate income.

CASH BASIS ACCOUNTING– Income is recorded when cash is received and expenses are recorded when cash is paid out.

CURRENT ASSET– An asset that is expected to last or be in use for less than one year.

DEMOGRAPHICS– Specific factors which distinguish a target population or market.

EQUITY– Ownership interest or claim of stock of a company, or funds contributed by the owners plus retained earnings or minus accumulated losses.

LIQUIDITY PATH– The route taken by a company allowing its owners to convert their ownership into currency.

P/L STATEMENT– Also known as the Income Statement, showing how well a company is doing (regarding profits and losses).

VENTURE CAPITALIST– An investor who supports small companies or provides capital to startup ventures that could not otherwise obtain financing.

Social Media Terms

API– (Application Programming Interface) gives users the ability to get a data feed source into their own blog or websites in real time.

APP– A term generally used when speaking about an application that will function on your computer, mobile, or handheld device.

BLOG– An online journal (or web log) that's updated with posts that show in reverse chronological order.

CAMPAIGN– A group of arranged marketing messages, with a staggered delivery, with a specific objective.

CLOUD COMPUTING– Users access data from anywhere rather than being tied to a specific device or machine.

CREATIVE COMMONS– A not-for-profit licensing system offering ways in which non-copyright holders may use copyrighted works.

CROWDFUNDING– A way to solicit donations from online users who collectively raise money to fund a project.

CROWDSOURCING– The act of obtaining ideas, work, or content from online users who collectively help solve the problem at hand.

EBOOK– An electronic version of a printed book that can be downloaded from a digital source and read on a computer, mobile device, or e-reader.

HASHTAG– (#) A way to tag social media posts by prefixing a word with the hash symbol, otherwise known as the number sign.

MICROBLOGGING– Short messages, usually shared on social media sites (for example, Twitter, which is 140 characters). Also known as microsharing.

PAID SEARCH MARKETING (PPC)– The placement of paid ads for a business or service on a search engine results page. If someone clicks the ad, an advertiser will pay the host for the click.

SEO– Arranging your website and web content to ensure it will appear close to the top of search engine rankings. Optimizing can include content keyword strategy and creating an intuitive web layout.

TAGS– Keywords to help users find searchable topics

TROLLS– Social media users that make rude, unwarranted statements with the intent to provoke others.

TWEEP– A Twitter user.

TWEET– A real-time post on the social media site Twitter.

TWEETUP– An organized or unorganized group of people that include the hashtag #TweetUp #SFTweetUp in their tweets, usually this group wants to accomplish a specific goal or spread a message.

VIRAL– Information that is circulated rapidly on the Internet.

APPENDIX A

Helpful Apps and Websites:

Download this page as a PDF: http://bit.ly/1QTxj2b

PRODUCTIVITY

- » Stop Procrastinating (StopProcrastinatingApp.com): An app to help you avoid distracting websites.
- » Cold Turkey (GetColdTurkey.com): An app that you can use to temporarily block yourself from distracting websites.
- » Klok (GetKlok.com): Time-tracking software for projects and miscellaneous task.
- » RescueTime.com: Tracks what you do with your time.
- » Freedom (MacFreedom.com): Apple app that can block you from the Internet for up to eight hours at a time.

ORGANIZATION

- » Cozi.com: Automatic appointment reminders via text messaging.

» Wunderlist.com: The best list tracking and to-do app that you can access from anywhere.
» Trello.com: A very visual app for managing all of your projects.
» Pocket (GetPocket.com): Save articles and videos for later reading.
» Mail To Self: Quickly email anything to yourself with a single tap. Available in iTunes for the iPhone and iPad.

APPOINTMENT SETTING

» TimeTrade.com - To make appointments with clients (consulting, coaching, etc.).
» Squareup.com/appointments: Online scheduling tool offered by Square, Inc.
» Doodle.com: A great way to determine what's the best time to make an appointment (this works really well for board meetings, strategy sessions, etc.).
» ScheduleOnce.com: This scheduling tool integrates with third parties such as Outlook, Infusionsoft, GoToMeeting, and WebEx.

More appointment-setting apps (some also integrate with Facebook via a tab):

» vCita
» Appointy
» SetMore
» Schedulicity

SOCIAL MEDIA MANAGEMENT:

» Buffer.com

» Dlvr.it (Post your blog content to all of your social media channels at the same time.)

» Friends+Me (FriendsPlus.Me)

» Hootsuite.com

» MavSocial.com

» MeetEdgar.com

» SocialOomph.com

» SproutSocial.com

» Zapier: Create an automated task (also see If this, then that at iftt.com for task automation).

WEBCASTING, TELESEMINAR, AND SCREEN SHARING:

» InstantTeleseminar.com: Teleseminars and webcasts.

» GoToWebinar.com: HD video conferencing with polls and surveys capabilities.

» ReadTalk.com: Web, audio, and video conferencing.

» GoToMeeting.com: Personal meeting rooms with screen sharing and audio.

» MeetingBurner.com: Screen sharing, teleconferencing, and more. Facebook and AWeber integrations, and email reminders set this service apart from competitors.

» Zoho.com/meeting: Web conferencing that can be embedded on your blog.

» WebEx.com: Web conferencing services with a training center and support center option for your audience.

» Yuuguu.com: Securely share your screen with anyone.

» Jing (Techsmith.com/jing.html): Take a screenshot and easily annotate it.

MISC.

» Canva.com: A drag and drop tool to design graphics for blog posts, social media banners, and much more.

» Quozio.com: Instantly make customizable quotes.

» GoToMyPC (GoToMyPC.com): Connect to your PC or Mac desktop from anywhere, from any device.

» Skype: Speak, see, and instant message anyone with this service.

» Spaxtel.com: When Skype is sketchy, this service will allow you to make quality phone calls via callback.

» F.lux (JustGetFlux.com): Prevent eye trouble and sleeping disruptions with this software that automatically adjusts the color of your computer's display to the time of day.

» Xero.com: Online accounting and bookkeeping solutions.

» QR code generator (QRstuff.com): Free QR code generator.

» CopyTalk.com: Use your voice to dictate a message and then the text will be sent to you via email.

» FullContact.com: Connect your email and address books and FullContact will automatically unify everything into one record (social links are integrated for relationship building).

APPENDIX B

Suggested Reading List
Download this list as a PDF: http://bit.ly/1QTxYRk

The Success Principles: How to Get from Where You are to Where You Want to Be by Jack Canfield

The 4-Hour Workweek: Escape 9-5, Live Anywhere, and Join the New Rich by Tim Ferriss

The 7-Day Startup by Dan Norris

The Art of Non-Conformity: Set Your Own Rules, Live the Life You Want, and Change the World by Chris Guillebeau

The $100 Startup: Reinvent the Way You Make a Living, Do What You Love, and Create a New Future by Chris Guillebeau

The Entrepreneur Mind: 100 Essential Beliefs, Characteristics, and Habits of Elite Entrepreneurs by Kevin Johnson

Why We Want You to be Rich by Donald Trump and Robert T. Kiyosaki

The Power of Who: You Already Know Everyone You Need to Know by Bob Beaudine

#Girl Boss by Sophia Amoruso

Getting Things Done: The Art of Stress-Free Productivity by David Allen

Jab, Jab, Jab Right Hook: How to Tell Your Story in a Noisy Social World by Gary Vaynerchuk

Thinking, Fast and Slow by Daniel Kahneman

Awakening the Giant Within by Tony Robbins

Unmarketing: Stop Marketing. Start Engaging. by Scott Stratten

The Sales Bible by Jeffrey Gitomer

Purple Cow: Transform Your Business by Being Remarkable by Seth Godin

How to Win Friends and Influence People by Dale Carnegie

The 7 Habits of Highly Effective People by Stephen R. Covey

Think and Grown Rich by Napoleon Hill

The Tipping Point: How Little Things Can Make a Big Difference by Malcolm Gladwell

Rich Dad, Poor Dad by Robert T. Kiyosaki

Influence: The Psychology of Persuasion by Robert B. Cialdini, PhD

The E-Myth Revisited by Michael E. Gerber

StrenghtsFinder 2.0 by Tom Rath

The Art of the Start: The Time-Tested, Battle-Hardened Guide for Anyone Starting Anything by Guy Kawasaki

The Lean Startup: How Today's Entrepreneurs Use Continuous Innovation to Create Radically Successful Businesses by Eric Ries

The Ten-Day MBA: A Step-By-Step Guide to Mastering the Skills Taught in America's Top Business Schools by Steven Silbiger

The Artist's Way by Julia Cameron

The War of Art by Steven Pressfield

Rightsizing Your Life by Ciji Ware

Enough: Finding More By Living With Less by Will Davis Jr.

ACKNOWLEDGEMENTS

I would like to extend sincere thanks to my friend AK Turner. Your writing advice is always appreciated and your humor really spices up my life. To my dear friend Rochelle, thank you for all of your years of friendship and fun. To my friend Diane, thank you for always helping me out even when you have so much on your plate already. To my lovely mother N. Katie, thank you for always being kind and supportive and for helping out around the house! I really appreciate you. To my step-dad Larry, thank you for being an amazing mentor to me and to my family. I am truly blessed to have you in my life. Even though I dedicated this book to my husband and children, I would again like to acknowledge how thankful I am for you. I am a very lucky lady.

To the Treasure Valley Critiquers: Loni, Dani, Camelyn, Jim, Troy, Marlie, Kelley, Angela, Brian, Carla, Cathy, and Anne, thank you for your years of friendship and encouragement.

I am very grateful for my amazing and very talented editor, Elizabeth Day. Thank you!

CONNECT WITH CHRISTY AND WIN A GIFT CARD FOR YOUR FAIR REVIEW.

If you enjoyed this book, please consider posting a review on Amazon.com. It may or may not increase your chances of finding good fortune but it will certainly make you a VIP to me! I hold monthly drawings for people who post a review. Simply send an email with a link to your review to: treasurevalleywriter@gmail.com.

If you want to connect with me virtually, please visit:

Website: http://the9to5escape.com

Facebook: Facebook.com/ChristyHoveyBooks

Google+: Plus.google.com/+ChristyHovey

Goodreads: Goodreads.com/ChristyHovey

Twitter: Twitter.com/ChristyHovey

Pinterest: Pinterest.com/ChristyHovey

Instagram: @The9to5EscapeArtist
Tag me on Instagram with a picture of you holding my book to be entered into my monthly gift card drawings.

Sign up to receive my monthly tips and tricks e-Newsletter and notifications of my upcoming books by visiting: http://eepurl.com/blwMp5